D1631504

NORFOLK COLLEGE LIBRARY

3 8079 00055 381 8

Growing Alpines
in Raised Beds, Troughs and Tufa

The Rock Gardener's Library also includes:

A Manual of Alpine and Rock Garden Plants
Edited by Christopher Grey-Wilson

A Guide to Rock Gardening
Richard Bird

The Alpine House
Robert Rolfe

The Propagation of Alpine Plants and Dwarf Bulbs
Brian Halliwell

Alpines in the Open Garden
Jack Elliott

Duncan Lowe

Growing Alpines
in Raised Beds, Troughs and Tufa

B. T. Batsford Limited · London

First published 1991

© Duncan Lowe, 1991

Line illustrations by the Author

All rights reserved. No part of this publication may be
reproduced, in any form or by any means, without permission
from the Publisher

Typeset by Paston Press, Loddon, Norfolk

Printed and bound in Great Britain by Biddles Ltd, Guildford

Published by
B. T. Batsford Ltd
4 Fitzhardinge Street
London W1H 0AH

A catalogue record for this book is available from the British
Library

ISBN 0 7134 7018 6

Contents

Colour Plates

Figures

Introduction

My search for more knowledge and understanding of alpines has filled my bookshelves and taken me to glorious places in the mountains. Slowly it became apparent, that to build a rock garden mimicking an Alpine slope might give great satisfaction to *me*, but not necessarily to the plants I wanted to grow there. As a result, the design and creation of each new garden featured less and less rocks and more specially prepared beds.

During those years I gradually acquired a collection of troughs, some of them centuries-old relics, others 'manufactured'. They have all moved with me, from garden to garden, first to a windy hillside in the Pennines, then to the moist Cheshire Plain and finally have come to rest in a placid river valley near the north-west coast. In addition to the troughs, hundreds of plants went along, housed temporarily in pots, but destined for beds that were still just shapes on a garden plan. Those beds are now more than ten years old and heavily populated with both old favourites and new introductions from far-away mountains.

Although the contents of this book are based primarily on these experiences they are also owing, in some measure, to the happy and productive friendships made over the years with others similarly engrossed in the pleasures and tribulations of growing alpines.

In my early days of growing alpines I carefully saved the label of every plant that died under my care, but by the time they had half-filled a bucket I was becoming somewhat discouraged and cremated the whole lot on the bonfire! Thirty years and three gardens later, I still pull out these sad little plastic epitaphs, but I hope that if I were to save them again, it would take longer to fill a bucket.

Acknowledgements
For contributions to the photographic illustrations I am indebted to the Royal Botanic Garden Edinburgh, the Alpine Garden Society, Mr W. Kirby, Mr A. Evans (RBG Edinburgh), M. and H. Taylor and Mr D. F. Mowle.

1 What is an alpine?

Almost any plant or shrub that is dwarf, hardy and perennial, is labelled 'alpine' in today's gardening. It is quite common to find flowers of the Swiss Alps, American Prairies and Greek Islands sharing the same rock-garden bed. Those who oppose such lumping together and strive for clearer definition, might describe an alpine plant as 'one that is native to the alpine zone of a mountain range'. Even this precision falters, however, if set against the fact that quite a number of mountain species occur naturally, elsewhere, at lower levels. For example, by the shores of Alaskan lakes, near to sea-level, grow tough little cushion- and mat-forming plants which, further south, are only to be found on the screes of lofty mountains.

Understandably, the gardener, loath to disqualify a host of suitable plants because they fail to comply with some disputed definition, has taken a generous approach, welcoming a great variety of species from many habitats, requiring only that they fit in with the scale and purpose of the rock garden and calling them all, for want of a better word, 'alpines'.

Even so, the majority are true mountain dwellers or natives of similar harsh environments and to help us to help them, in cultivation, a knowledge of how they live in their natural homes is invaluable. Perhaps the best way to pursue that knowledge is to slowly and thoughtfully climb the mountain, from tree-line to snow-line, looking at things with a gardener's eye and trying to understand the needs and the preferences of the plants that make their homes in those wild places.

In the relatively rich earth of the lower slopes there are some immediately familiar herbaceous plants, adopted by gardeners long ago and now established as border plants. Geranium, trollius, aconite and delphinium, for instance, are not regarded as alpines, but they certainly grow on alps, those humpy meadows leading to the flanks of the mountain, and it is on those flanks that a definite change in the vegetation takes place. The ground becomes stony and the underlying rock is bared here and there, weathered into blunted outcrops, lichen-covered and offering homes to a few lower-altitude crevice plants. There is still soil here on these steep slopes, but it is thinner and poorer than that of the meadows.

With the gain in height comes less genial weather and as a result, the plants are altered in character. Tall flower spikes and long leaves are too vulnerable to the stronger winds, and roots must delve deeply to give a firm hold. Other than in sheltered crannies and small hollows, there is full exposure to everything that the weather can bring and flowers rise little above huddled foliage. Grass is still

11

plentiful, but it is wiry and short, giving way to stone slides in places but generally stabilising the stony soil to give anchorage for some of the best-loved alpine plants, like gentians, soldanellas and primulas. The very steepness of the ground and the stones and grit incorporated in it, ensure that the drainage is absolute. No puddles here after a heavy shower; the excess water runs away downhill or percolates through the rock and debris beneath the turf.

Before climbing further, to explore habitats where soil is scarce or almost non-existent, it is useful to pause and consider mountain soils. They have not had the scientific attention given to the agricultural soils of the plains and low hills, presumably because they are not used to grow food. Whilst there are mountain regions where precarious rice paddies and cereal patches are terraced on slopes, these are man-made and have been built up and maintained over centuries. What little is known, however, is helpful to the grower of alpines.

Mountain soils contain very little nitrogen and their vegetation has evolved to make do with tiny quantities, to such an extent that some of the plants can be physically poisoned by levels that would be ideal in our vegetable gardens. The traces that do exist are assumed to come from fragments of organic matter and to a greater degree from rainwater, particularly that of thunderstorms. In contrast, some minerals can be more abundant than they are in the lowlands. Potassium (potash) is frequently present at much higher levels, particularly where granite prevails, and in limestone areas calcium is plentiful. The source of these minerals is the outcome of the perpetual breaking-down and pulverising of the rocks by heat and cold and the slow but steady erosion by rain and melting snow.

The presence of air and hence oxygen, in the stony, free-draining soils is high in comparison with garden soil and this could be important to the health of the plants, in discouraging fungal attack on roots and aiding their take-up of nutrients.

Air spaces are also essential to good drainage; they form the escape channels for excess water and as they empty, draw down air, refreshing the oxygen supplies and sustaining beneficial organisms in the soil.

In certain patches on mountain sides there are well-drained 'wet' soils, an awkward description which seems to hold a contradiction but is nevertheless true. Often called 'flushes', they occur where spring or melt-water is pushed up to the surface. Such places attract plants like pinguiculas that demand an unfailing copious supply of moisture at their roots. The difference between these patches and soggy spots in the garden is that on the mountain the water is always on the move, fresh, cool and aerated, only passing through on its way to the valley. There is no lingering pool of stale water, yet the ground never dries out, a condition that is virtually impossible to reproduce in the garden unless blessed with a permanent stream or spring; even then it never seems to work like the real thing.

So much, then, for the stony slopes and their coverings and on to the high places, which begin where the turf surrenders to stone-slides and crags

12

buttressing the summit. The climb crosses screes which at first sight appear to be devoid of all plant life. These fan out from the bases of gullies in the cliffs or pile up below walls of rock and are of two types. The first is the 'live' scree which is still being supplied with shattered rock from above, whereas the second type has lost this feed and is at rest, in which state it is described as 'consolidated'.

Even on the unstable 'live' scree, there are, remarkably, just a few plants that have evolved sufficiently to survive around the quieter edges. Some of these are nomadic, staying only long enough in one spot to take up what little sustenance is there, then moving on, by stolons, roots or seed and leaving behind their dead remains. Campanulas, violets and poppies are typical of these 'rock-hoppers'. Others, like thlaspies and geums, send down long, tough thongs of root deep into the scree and hang on, capable to some extent of moving and stretching with minor shifts of the rubble.

In comparison with the live scree, the consolidated type has a much larger and diverse plant population. The settled heap of debris is no longer bombarded with fresh fragments from above or disturbed by periodic downhill slides and is soon host to the first primitive plant forms. Algae coats the surface stones and in due course is followed by lichens. As time passes, mosses begin to spread and leave their remains in small crannies to form a moisture-retentive substance that is far from being soil, but sufficient, when combined with dust and sand, to give a 'toe-hold' to more advanced plant forms. By such progression the scree is gradually populated, albeit sparsely, with a variety of plant species specially adapted to the terrain, many of which, in bloom, are amongst the finest of the mountain flowers.

Cushion- and mat-forming plants predominate on the screes, exploring with their long roots to secure reliable moisture supplies and making full use of every scrap of nutritious material encountered. They demonstrate well the highly evolved nature of mountain plants, whose abilities to seek out food and water and efficiency in using these, are comparable with those of desert species. There is an important difference, however, between the two, that should be noted by the gardener, which is that with only one or two exceptions, those adapted to mountain rocks and screes are not equipped to hold a reserve of water within their tissues and will perish if their moisture supplies fail for only a short time.

The other form of stone heap met with on the mountain is the moraine, which although formed by a quite different action, associated with glacial movement, is very similar to scree in structure and consequently the plant types that it attracts. Earlier in this present century 'moraine beds' were often a prized feature of the enthusiast's rock garden, incorporating below-surface pipework to irrigate the root-runs. It was obviously understood then, that although the surface of a scree or moraine suggests that the whole thing is arid, there is in fact persistent moisture present not far below to sustain the plants that have chosen to live there. This can be difficult to believe when slithering across the dusty pebbles in the heat of an Alpine summer day, but it must be remembered that snow-melt, rainfall, low cloud and dew all contribute to sustaining the moisture content held below the insulating surface debris.

Above the screes and up to the summer snow-line, the climber discovers crevice plants, rooting into rock fissures in the buttresses and ridges. For good reasons many of these, the toughest of all alpines, have adopted the cushion form of growth, often with hair-fine root systems of great length, ideal for exploiting the narrowest of cracks. They are equipped to take up whatever traces of nutrient are encountered and to tap any meagre water catchment discovered, which is often just a film of moisture coating the deep, inner walls of the fault.

The fine-rooted species could be regarded as the best-adapted types, being able to make use of a wide variety of crack forms, including those in layers of shale. There are other cushion species which employ a tap-root as both anchor and feeder, but this imposes greater limits on the narrowness of the fissure the plant can utilise.

The alternative growth form favoured by some crevice dwellers is the tight, flat mat, again using either thread-like roots or a rugged tap form. Both the mat and the domed cushion present low resistance to strong winds, keeping down the strain on their anchorages and just as importantly, minimising any drying or freezing effects. The two shapes also allow melting snow and shuttering stones to pass over them with least damage. Even in bloom the same crouching habit is maintained, the flowers sitting close to the foliage. Hairiness in many of the species is another defence against the wind, slowing evaporation and holding a thin insulating layer of air over the leaf surfaces.

Not all crevice plants are confined to the higher altitudes, however, they are found at all levels, right down to coasts where sea-pinks stud the shore cliffs and tufts of soapwort cling to the walls of road cuttings. In such locations the plants are often looser and taller, but their stature and habit still admit them to the rock garden; after all, they are rock plants.

The purpose of these first few pages has been to determine the special nature of alpines and to look for indications, in their natural homes, of what might be their special needs as cultivated plants. A summing-up will serve to establish some guidelines for creating various garden constructions and plantings.

Drainage

The thin stony soils skinning the mountain slopes drain rapidly. On the rocks and screes the run-off is even faster but enough moisture is retained, deep in the crevices and beneath the surfaces, to sustain the root-runs during dry periods. After the snow cover has melted away, showers, thunderstorms and low cloud act regularly to top up the reserves.

A heap of coarse gravel or stone chippings would have just the right structure to give the immaculate drainage that alpines, and particularly scree plants, enjoy. A few of the very spartan species might be cultivated on such a heap, but on the whole it would fail to retain sufficient moisture or hold enough nutrients to satisfy most plants for very long. Submerged pipes could supply a steady trickle of water, supplemented at times with liquid feed, but such a system would approach a horticultural intensive-care unit, with no place in a garden.

It is perhaps sufficient to note that alpines detest stale, soggy conditions, but must have consistent fresh moisture supplies and that many are likely to suffer from drought earlier than other garden plants.

Light

Very few mountain plants seek shade and whilst they are often to be found favouring north-facing ground, they are still fully exposed to the sun. The northerly slope just receives sunlight at a gentler angle and so heats up and dries out less quickly. As a result it is less likely to parch in dry periods.

Other features of mountain light are important to the grower. In the sun, even at high altitudes, it can feel very hot, but the air temperature is far lower than it is in the valleys below, hence the description of Alpine resorts as 'invigorating'. Hot, oppressive, humid conditions are much more prevalent at low levels and rarely afflict wild alpine plants. Another difference between the plains and the heights is the quality of the sunlight; as the air thins with altitude it lets through more ultra-violet light and this could be important to those plants that dwell in high places.

Food

There is very little nitrogen in mountain soils, however, there is a compensating richness in some other plant nutrients, but generally speaking, alpines have to work hard for their food, which is rarely abundant. In cultivation, treating them to a 'wholesome' diet is doing them no favours; they are not equipped to deal with it and, if not actually damaged by the excess, may respond by producing gross foliage and few flowers. Why bother to strive for procreation when the living is easy?

It should be sufficient to ensure that in the garden the alpine plants receive modest amounts of food, with low nitrogen content. Clean air, sunshine and well-aerated soil go a long way to meeting their needs.

Growth and rest

In the wild, mountain plants have a growing season that is considerably shorter than that enjoyed by plants in easier climates. They emerge from the slush of melting snow between late May and early July, and have until the onset of October to grow, bloom, set seed, ripen and make ready for winter. Three months or so to accomplish what our garden plants do in a leisurely seven or eight!

On the other hand, the alpines don't awake to an uncertain spring with false starts, dry spells, late frosts etc. They are greeted by summer sunshine and the

15

whole environment is fresh and buoyant. Alpine vegetation responds vigorously; plants in the turf race to form their leaves and raise their flowers before the grass overshadows them. On the screes and rocks there is the same hurry to develop in the brief summer of the heights.

Before the hard frosts can reach them, many alpines are covered by the first snows. They then hibernate, blanketed by cold, crisp ice crystals, at an even temperature, safe from gales, fogs, pests and diseases, in the dark. A few species do not enjoy such comfort. On exposed ridges and rock faces those that live in the crevices must endure everything that the mountain winter can produce, but in both cases the plants are truly dormant, their life forces reduced to just enough for survival, awaiting a signal from strength of light, temperature or day length, to trigger the cycle for another year.

Down to earth

A comparison of the conditions in the wild with those of the garden reveals how incredible it is that any of the mountain-dwelling species can be persuaded to even tolerate a life in cultivation. In an urban plot, the crisp clear air of the heights is replaced by an atmosphere laced with sulphur, exhaust fumes, lead and the fall-out from local industries. Although country gardens enjoy some improvement, the pollution is still present to a lesser degree. The low-altitude air is also denser, screening more of the sunlight and diluting its quality.

Other differences separate the natural and the garden climates. Lowland winters are often variable, wavering between near-Arctic cold and mild 'false springs'. Today's snowfall can be tomorrow's flood. Biting frosts and cold, dry winds find no barrier of deep snow between them and the resting plants. Weeks before spring is truly beginning a freak in the weather pattern can produce a mild spell, turning February into April and sending urgent signals to buds and roots that it is time to move. This lack of consistency in the winter period prevents the plants from becoming fully dormant; their sleep is disturbed and they are attacked by the elements. Not surprisingly they suffer.

In the season of growth they suffer again, from a new set of enemies. Depending on the local climate where they are being grown, they can experience summers that are hot and dry, cool and wet, dull and humid or some alternations between these, all of which are very un-Alpine. In addition, the plants are attacked by slugs, snails, aphids, root-eaters, leaf-miners, moulds and viruses, few of which they have ever encountered in their natural lives and so have never developed defences against them.

There is no way yet of vaccinating our plants against disease. There is no satisfactory substitute for snow-cover. Nothing much can be done to improve the sunlight, where it is lacking, and sophisticated watering systems are beyond the means or ingenuity of most growers. It is left to the skill of the gardener to contrive places and conditions that will fulfil, as far as possible, the essential requirements of the plants.

16

Trials and experiments, carried out by many growers, have confirmed that attempts to provide replicas of the natural growing places do not necessarily produce the best results in cultivation. Take, for example, the case of the crevice plant. The difficulties entailed in building, planting and maintaining garden versions of fissures in mountain rock are discussed later, but is it essential to provide a crevice for a crevice plant? In nature the plant is confined to stony perches not because of an inability to live anywhere else, but perhaps because it has been driven there by competitors. More vigorous or aggressive species dominate the 'easier' ground below the cliff or boulder and so, to survive, the crevice plant has probably evolved to make the best of what is offered by a crack in the rock that would not support the lustier competitors.

Where the competitors and predators are kept at bay by the gardener, the plant from the rocky refuge might enjoy a less frugal living place, provided that the conditions are not too far removed from those to which it is so specially adapted. If we create a perfectly drained root-run, containing a very modest amount of sustenance and a water-shedding, quick-drying surface upon which the plant can sit or sprawl, perhaps it will react favourably — and quite often it does.

Such compromises have led to success with many species that the conventional, soil-filled rock garden has failed to satisfy. Raised beds, troughs and tufa are leading examples of the means by which we persuade highly adapted plants from unique habitats to accept life in the garden. They have brought permanent changes to the cultivation of rock-garden plants and are at the heart of what is to follow.

2 Raised beds

Prepared plots of soil raised above the general ground level are by no means a recent development in cultivation. Back in the sixteenth century, gardeners were aware of the benefits to be gained from raised beds and used them to grow herbs and certain food crops requiring something better than ordinary garden conditions. Raised beds were frequently used in the formalised layouts of stately homes to carry through the architectural themes into the surrounding grounds, and create areas for special plantings.

The rock gardener has adopted the same device much more recently, recognising the basic virtues of providing a special place, with special features for special plants.

There is no such thing as the 'ideal' raised bed; they are built in many styles and materials and are filled with various soil mixtures to suit garden design, plant types, local climate etc. Limitations of space, spare time, funds and sheer energy, can all influence the shape, size and make-up of raised beds, but the same ground rules apply to all of them.

Choice of site

In British gardens, beds containing alpines need all the light they can get. Sunny beds do entail more watering chores during hot spells, but to reduce the watering needs by the use of shading is to deprive the plants of something they need in quantity to give of their best. Even in the hottest and driest counties of the UK, therefore, the raised bed should occupy an open place in full light, unless of course it is intended for plants that naturally require some shade, such as woodlanders.

In countries where the summers consistently produce prolonged periods of more intense sunlight and high air temperatures, it may be necessary to temper the sunlight somewhat. In such cases slatted shades are used and have the effect of rationing the sunlight rather than diluting it, retaining the quality but reducing the quantity. There is little that can be done about high air temperatures other than siting the bed where the air currents are lively. A breezy spot can be excellent, but if the breezes develop into icy, dehydrating gales in the winter months, these can cripple and even kill some of the alpine species accustomed to a sheltering snow blanket.

Even if the natural drainage of the garden is first-class, there is a source of unwanted moisture that must be avoided, and that is the drip from overhanging branches and foliage. The water droplets can carry all manner of blights onto the plants below, and particularly in the winter months, will cause great distress to the plants, leading to rot and decay.

Another effect of nearby trees and large shrubs can lurk undetected. Whilst the bed may be positioned clear of their overhanging boughs, it may still be near enough for their roots to infiltrate and they like nothing more than to grow up into the carefully prepared bed filling. Just to be sure that this does not happen, it is wise to dig one or two exploratory holes.

The fortunate garden has naturally good drainage, but many are not fortunate, or at least have problem areas. If the bed is built where water lies long, or in a permanently soggy area, the bed filling can behave like a wick, drawing up water and maintaining a sour, clammy state, even though it is higher than the surrounding earth. If such places cannot be avoided, drains must be installed with a run-off to a lower level.

Mundane matters can also influence the selection of the best site: children's favourite play spots, the dog's run, the place where the paper-boy props his bike, and of course, the washing line! A careless infant foot can tear out the firmest tap-root, and a wayward flapping bed sheet can decapitate a whole colony of flowers. Further important consideration is the character of the garden around the chosen site. Close to a building, formal beds can complement the architecture. Against less formal backgrounds there is scope for more rustic constructions and relaxed forms. In woodland or ericaceous schemes it is enjoyable to depart from hard materials altogether and to create walls with logs, thick boughs or peat blocks, though the latter are not easy to make stable or to maintain in good condition for any length of time.

If the only site available is shaded it can still be worth while to build a bed, in order to achieve the drainage and elevation, accepting that it will only please selected plants which either enjoy or tolerate limited direct sunlight. It is quite practical to build a bed against an existing wall, by adding two sides and a front, and if the existing wall is tall, it can be blended and softened with restrained climbing plants, such as alpine clematis and dwarf ivy.

Size

There is no real limit to the size of a raised bed; it could go on like Hadrian's great work, but there are functional considerations that affect some of the dimensions. Unless it is of huge proportions the bed will be planted, maintained and enjoyed from the sides, so its width is important. If the centre of the bed can be comfortably reached from either side, it is a great benefit. This limits the width to no more than 1.5m ($4\frac{1}{2}$ft). If this is exceeded the gardener is overreaching and using one hand to prevent a face-down collapse onto the surface.

From several points of view the ideal height would be around waist level, allowing easy reaching and bringing the plants, their flowers and their scents closer for full appreciation. Such elevation can increase involvement and

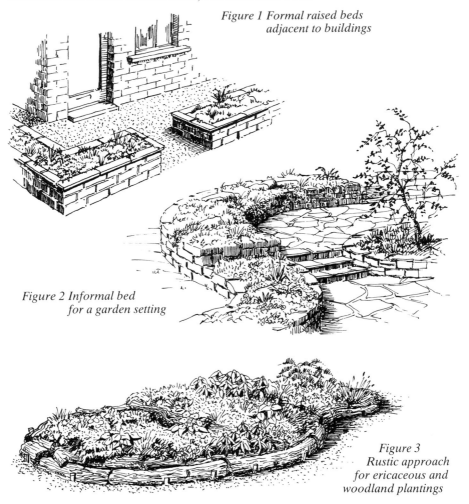

*Figure 1 Formal raised beds
adjacent to buildings*

*Figure 2 Informal bed
for a garden setting*

*Figure 3
Rustic approach
for ericaceous and
woodland plantings*

enjoyment for those who are disabled and more will be said of this later. With increases in height, however, come added problems, in structural strength, filling, costs and manpower.

Experiments have confirmed that a minimum height of 25cm (10in) is sufficient to provide an adequately drained and sufficiently deep root-run for the majority of rock-garden plants. Such low-level versions are the easiest (and cheapest) to build and fill, but involve more back-bending than the taller ones.

The filling is a very important consideration when deciding upon the overall size. It is a sobering fact that a simple bed, measuring 2m long, 1m wide and 0.5m high ($6\frac{1}{2}$ft × 3ft × $1\frac{1}{2}$ft) will require about 1000kg (1tonne) of filling mixture. Furthermore, this material must first be thoroughly blended before it is shovelled in and the physical work entailed can be compared with that required to mix a similar quantity of concrete.

Material costs can be a powerful restraint on the planning of dimensions, especially if natural stone is the chosen material. If a reasonable soil is not readily available and the filling must be made-up from bought materials, this can be a considerable expense.

Preparing the site

Before building starts, the whole of the area upon which the bed will stand should be thoroughly cleared of all perennial weeds. It is amazing how persistent dandelions, docks and bindweed can be and how far they can sprout upwards when buried. Old stumps and roots should be removed completely, as they can harbour several nuisances, not least of which are various fungi, which may suddenly appear, decorating the bed with toadstools, long after completion and planting.

A particular bit of questionable advice, which keeps appearing in many gardening publications, is the recommendation to dig a shallow pit and to fill this with rubble to form a well-drained base for a rock garden or bed. Why should a pit take water away if the ground will not? If underlying sand or gravel is revealed when the pit is dug, then it would make sense, but if not, all that has been created is a sump that will hold stagnant water.

Drainage must be fully effective and long-lasting if it is needed. Baked clay field-drain pipes or the perforated plastic types are the surest means of leading surplus water away to a run-off or existing drain. These need not be deeply buried, but should be laid on a bed of coarse sand or grit and covered with the same to prevent silting-up by soil and debris.

So far, a more or less level site has been assumed, but the raised-bed principle can be adapted to slopes and the construction is no more difficult. The front or downhill-facing wall is the main feature (Figure 4). Preparation is a matter of cutting one or more level 'terraces' into the slope and building on these. It is difficult to produce anything less than superb drainage with the fall of the slope assisting so much.

Foundations

For random or field-stone walling the foundations need only be minimal; little more than a levelling and firming of the earth. Nothing more than this is done in authentic drystone work.

The more precise and formal walling requires a basic footing to give a solid base for the laying of blocks or bricks. In building terms the height and weight of raised-bed walling is very low and light foundations are quite sufficient. A shallow trench is dug out to follow the run of the wall, its width being a little more than that of the building blocks or bricks and to a depth of 10–15cm (4–6in). The trench is filled with a concrete mixture containing something like: 1 part cement, 2 parts sand and 4 parts stone chippings or shingle (the proportions are not critical). Sufficient of the mix should be used to bring it

21

Figure 4 Terracing with raised beds

level with or just below the prepared surface of the site. Two days' setting time is sufficient before building work can be started.

Care taken in preparing foundations is repaid in the laying of the all-important first course. With the aid of a straight board and a spirit-level the wet concrete can be smoothed and levelled quite easily.

It is not necessary to build beds on newly prepared ground; they can be erected on existing solid surfaces forming ready-made foundations. This option gives the opportunity to make use of an old concrete building base, add a feature to a terrace or patio, or even to flank a driveway. The bed is simply built directly onto the surface in such cases, with care taken to incorporate plenty of generous drainage outlets in the bottom course of each wall to prevent any risk of waterlogging. To compensate for the solid base, the depth of the bed should exceed the minimum recommended earlier. About 0.5m (20in) should be sufficient, however, to give a satisfactory depth of root-run and enough bulk material to prevent rapid drying-out in hot spells. It is sometimes recommended that beds built in this manner should have a layer of coarse peat or composted bark placed in the bottom before filling, to combat drought conditions. Although this might be effective in regions with low rainfall it is likely to be too much of a good thing in wetter climates, by forming a persistently over-wet base that may seriously impede drainage.

There is another form of raised bed that requires a rather different foundation. Unlike those already discussed it does not sit on the ground, but is supported on pillars or piers. More will be said of this variation later, but the

22

foundations are confined to the bases of the supports and are prepared in a similar manner to the concrete-filled trench type.

Building materials

In the planning and construction of important garden features, natural stone is very often regarded as the ideal material. This inclination probably originates in gardening traditions, from early days when stone was relatively cheap and when wholly ornamental gardens were restricted to the estates of the well-to-do. Now there are millions of us, creating gardens in suburban plots, behind town houses and around country cottages, bursting with ideas and enthusiasm, but limited in time and funds. Alternatives to stone have been used, with good, bad and indifferent results.

The deliberate avoidance of stone or its imitations has already been mentioned in relation to situations where a bed joins, or is close to, existing brickwork or concrete. A bed built in matching or harmonising brick, or concrete walling blocks, can look more in keeping with such surroundings than the most beautiful stone. If the existing brick is of a harsh colour, a matching bed might be at odds with some of the flowers, in which case it would be better to use something with a neutral tone. There are building blocks available that do not attempt to imitate stone but have a textured surface, usually on just one face, and are tinted to overcome the drab grey of the cement used in their making. They can be criticised for being all of the same colour, but this ceases to be a defect when they are used, as in this case, to harmonise with similarly uniform walls and paths.

In some areas of Britain and elsewhere, brick-built houses are surfaced with stucco or pebble dash. It is unlikely that this type of finish would be weatherproof on bed walls; the lack of damp-proofing would lead to frost-flaking and peeling.

The makers of synthetic stone are steadily improving their product. Sometimes called 'reconstituted stone', the material usually simulates squared, dressed stone with a rough chiselled finish on one face and comes in a range of sizes and subdued colours. The sizes are often proportioned to allow patterned laying, as opposed to uniform courses of the same depth, and the finished effect can be quite pleasing. At a distance it is hard to be sure that it is artificial, particularly if a mix of tints has been used and weather stains have softened the general appearance.

The cast-concrete slabs used for the pavements of our towns and cities have been used with some success by resourceful gardeners. When cut into smaller rectangles these can be used as walling blocks and in time they will mellow a little, but that awful elephant-grey persists, unvaried throughout the whole wall. It is possible to remove some of the drabness by applying a stain and there are now commercial dyes available for this purpose. There is also a cheap home-made version, employing a substance familiar to gardeners as sulphate of iron (ferrous sulphate) which, dissolved in water, can be painted onto the dry

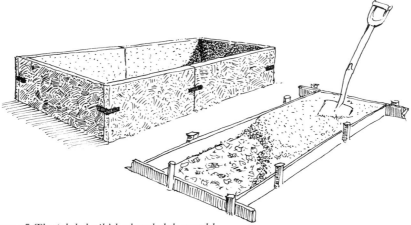

Figure 5 The 'slab-built' bed and slab mould

surface of the concrete to produce a permanent colouring. The tint achieved depends to some degree on the strength of the solution and the constituents of the concrete. At worst the final colour can be a vicious ginger and at best a reasonable buff. As the result takes a day or two to develop, a few prior trials are essential before treating anything of value. Concrete is again the basic material of a quite different method used to produce walls suitable for raised-bed constructions. In this little used, but quite valid process, the concrete is cast as slabs, which are subsequently joined up to form a bed. It is, to all intents and purposes, a prefabricated building system. Figure 5 illustrates the simple mould required and how the slab's outer surface can be embossed with an informal texture by laying various materials in the mould prior to the concrete filling. Twigs, foliage, crumpled paper, strips of bark etc. will produce textures, and when the concrete has set, can be brushed and scrubbed off, leaving their imprint on the face of the slab. The bed is made up using the slabs domino fashion, and either joining them with steel plates and bolts, or setting them in concrete in shallow trenches. It must be said that although the patterning does help to reduce the starkness of the finished structure, it might still look perhaps better suited to a cemetery than a garden. A similarly functional but unlovely device can be made from wooden railway sleepers laid edge to edge. However decorated it is unlikely to draw the envy of the neighbourhood.

Most types of house brick eventually flake and crumble when used to build garden features, although this may take several years with good quality facing brick. There are frost-proof bricks, intended for use below damp-proof courses and for engineering structures, but they are generally an unattractive colour and expensive. Concrete bricks, known in the building trade as 'concrete commons', are frost-proof and surprisingly cheap, a hundred or more costing less than a tankful of petrol for the family car.

Railway sleepers have been mentioned, though without much enthusiasm, as a timber alternative to solid, hard materials, but other lumber can be used to pleasing effect. Lengths of tree trunks or stout boughs, selected to nest well together, will form a low wall, supported discreetly with short posts driven into the ground (Figure 3). Of course the timber used should be naturally rot-resistant; oak, alder, elm and yew are good examples. Enclosures made in this manner suit the character of ericaceous or woodland plantings and can be expected to last many years. Logs used 'stockade' fashion get a mixed reaction from gardeners. Whilst they function very well, their 'organ pipe' uniformity can sit uneasily with other garden features. The outermost slices removed from logs at the sawmill look very attractive with their uneven edges and curved, bark-clad surfaces, but as long-term materials they are wanting. Being sap-wood they can warp alarmingly and will shed their bark covering as they weather. They also rot more quickly.

Now to stone, with all its colours and textures, its strength and its perma-nence. If cost is not a problem, or if stone is there to be (legally) picked up and used, why bother with anything else? Well, it may be that it just would not look right in certain styles of garden. The local rock may be difficult to work with or its colour might be harsh or drab. Otherwise stone is a wonderful material for creative and satisfying building. Other than the two most commonly used types (sandstone and granite), there are slates, limestones, mixed cobbles and flint nodules, all of which have been used, in their natural form or 'worked', to build walls.

The easiest type for the amateur to handle is dressed stone, already cut into regular-shaped blocks and hence relatively simple to lay. Freestone, taken as quarried without further work being done on it, requires more skill, but the finished wall is perhaps the closest in keeping with the character of the rock garden. River, sea-shore and field stones are less easy to marry and in most cases require far more mortar to hold them in place. Some slates cleave evenly and are a joy to use, whilst others will split every way but parallel, producing unhelpful angular lumps.

Construction methods and techniques

A little knowledge and skill in the trimming and cutting of stone and concrete is enormously helpful to the task of wall building, particularly if there are many odd, awkward shapes, or if using paving slabs as the basic material. The only tools required are a heavy hammer and a wide-bladed (Boaster) chisel. Figure 6 shows how these are used and the basic rules are:

Trimming   Never try to hack off a large piece in one go. Work progressively, with finger-thick bites. Always use a hard, firm surface as an anvil.

Cutting   Make a shallow chisel groove along the line of the intended cut. Stand the slab on edge and tap heavily up and down the cut line, *on the reverse side*.

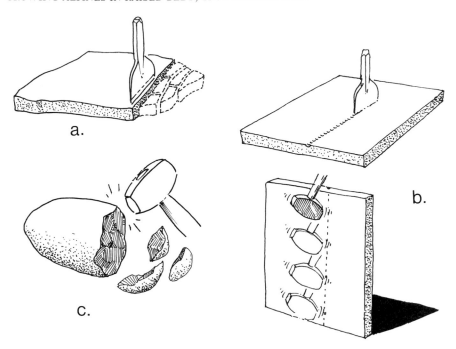

*Figure 6 Cutting and trimming **a**. trimming a stone or concrete slab **b**. cutting a paving slab **c**. knapping a rounded stone*

Wall building

Bricks and blocks   Assuming that the foundation has been laid reasonably level, the first course is all-important. Numerous DIY books and pamphlets explain the principles and steps involved in laying and bonding courses; all that need be stressed here is that a line and a spirit-level are absolutely essential to producing an acceptable finish. If there are any doubts about having the skill or strength for the work, or a disability imposes limits, there is often a professional in the neighbourhood who will do the job in an odd evening or weekend.

Dressed stone   It is unlikely that the gardener will have bought new dressed stone for bed building. As well as being costly, it is unnecessary, because certainly in Britain, reclaimed material is available and for the intended purpose is probably superior to the new, due to the weathering and mellowing it has undergone previously. Unless, as in some cases, it is all of one thickness, it is laid to give variation in the horizontal joints as well as staggering the verticals (Figure 7a). Otherwise the laying technique is very similar to that used for bricks and blocks.

Freestone   This is the type most frequently used for random or drystone walling and presents something of a challenge to the amateur, who tends to use all the best pieces first and ends up with a heap of oddly shaped chunks for the

*Figure 7 Walling types **a**. dressed stone walling **b**. freestone or random walling*

final courses. The skilled waller deliberately finds places for the awkward pieces as the work progresses (Figure 7b), even so there isn't a place for every stone. When assessing the amount of material required, an excess of about 20 per cent should be allowed for the stones that simply will not fit anywhere.

There are purists who insist that such walls should be built entirely without mortar to look their best. Personal experience has confirmed, however, that functionally these unbonded structures are unsatisfactory; a nudge with the wheelbarrow, 'frost heaving', settlement and other moderate disturbances can cause distortions and dislodgements. If the wall is not sufficiently stable to be walked along occasionally, it is not firm enough for its purpose.

Freestone walls can be strengthened in several ways. They can be fully mortared just as brick walls are, laying the stones on a bed of mortar and filling the vertical joints as each course is added, and cleaning off surplus with the trowel. Another, similar method, employs full mortaring, but has the joints raked out when the mortar is partially set, to emphasise the random pattern of the stones. 'Hidden' mortaring produces the drystone effect whilst giving strength and stability to the wall. These last two techniques are illustrated in Figure 8.

Cobbles and rounds   Some gardeners seem to have a natural skill for assembling oddly shaped stones into pleasing structures, perhaps stemming from hours spent with jigsaw puzzles or Leggo in earlier years. The Normans and others, raised great buildings, which still stand, using cobbles helped by a few heavy corner stones and a lot of mortar. There is much to be learned from these historic piles and from old farms and barns built mainly from field stones or river cobbles.

Knapping is used by professional wallers to aid the use of much-rounded stones. Taking the roughly egg-shaped lump, they knock off an end with one or two sharp blows from a heavy hammer, which produces a roughly flat face. The stone is then laid with the knapped end outermost, making it easier to achieve

27

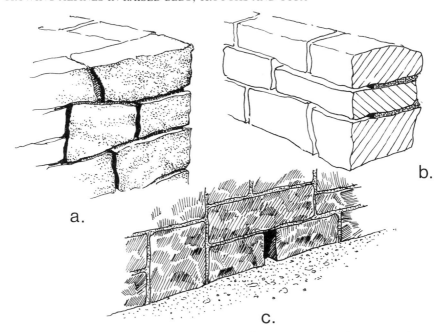

Figure 8 Walling methods **a**. *raked joints* **b**. *'hidden' mortaring* **c**. *drainage outlet*

an even finish to the wall. A generous amount of mortar is still required, but far less is exposed in the completed work than would be with round-ended stones. Figure 6 includes an illustration.

Granite sets, often and wrongly called cobbles, were used in the past to surface the roads of towns and cities. Asphalt has superseded them but they are still being dug out in road improvements and are often available to the public. Their colour varies very little and they are of a uniform shape and size, but if laid like bricks, with what was the rough-hewn base used as the outer face, they make a solid and attractive wall.

General points

Mortar Amateurs tend to use the same 3 to 1 sand/cement mixture for all jobs involving brick, blocks, paving or stone, unaware that for wall building this mix is richer than necessary. In the building trade mortar for laying can have five to six parts of sand to one of cement, not to cut costs, but to give the mortar the best properties for the job. Richer mixes are reserved for pointing and where hard surface finishes are required.

The pre-mixing of cement and sand, prior to adding the water, is very important to the quality of the final result. Wet or very damp sand will not mix thoroughly with the cement, and the end result will be patchy in strength and adhesion. The amount of water used depends to some extent on the nature and initial dampness of the sand. Water should be added gradually, with the mixing action going on all the time, until the mortar behaves something like mud. A

28

worthwhile aid is a wetting agent or 'plasticiser'. Added to the water it makes the mortar much easier to handle and control.

Corners   Where stone walls meet at right angles or where an abrupt change in direction occurs, large blocks should be used to give added strength and stability (Figure 7).

Drainage outlets   Escape channels for excess water are provided simply by leaving several vertical joints unmortared in the bottom course of the wall (see Figure 8).

Hidden mortaring   This method restricts the use of mortar to the inward part of the stone joints (see Figure 8) so that little or no mortar is visible on the wall's outer face. It is not recommended for the taller constructions, which require the strength of full mortaring.

Capping   In all types of wall, the final or top course should either be fully mortared or consist of long capping pieces bedded in mortar.

Table beds
Still essentially a raised bed, but of quite different construction, the table bed's main component is the slab that forms the elevated base. This is rarely a very large unit (the larger type having the spread of a billiard table) and is composed of several pieces. The slab is supported on pillars or piers and around its edges are low walls, usually 15–20cm high (6–9in). Heights exceeding this produce a top-heavy appearance, and when the bed is filled, the weight is tremendous. Figures 9 and 10 show two types, one of which incorporates a wide overhang feature that is helpful to wheelchair gardeners, giving knee room beneath the slab, enabling them to get much closer for working on the bed.

The thicker types of concrete paving, square or rectangular, are the simplest and cheapest means for making up the slab. Supports are positioned to suit the geometry of the pavings, so that they come centrally beneath the paving joints. A little bedding mortar is usually used just to aid the levelling-up of the pavings where they meet, but a slight gap should be left to provide the all-important drainage outlet.

As well as being used to form the base slab, pavings can also be utilised for the vertical supports. They are set in shallow trenches and adjusted with packings of stone fragments to be truly upright, level and all of one height. Concrete is then poured into the trenches to fix the structure. These slim pillars require a higher degree of accuracy in setting up than do built piers, but they are cheap and avoid a lot of brick or stone-laying work.

The pre-cast concrete sections sold as path or driveway edgings make ideal side pieces if bedded in mortar when they are set in place. Alternatively, bricks or dressed walling blocks, used on edge, will do equally well.

Figure 9 A table bed built on brick or stone piers

Filling the bed

Soil mixtures

To a large extent the make-up of the material used to fill the bed will depend upon the types of plant to be grown there. For specialised plantings, such as a collection of cushion saxifrages, the soil mixture would be specially prepared to suit their particular needs, whereas for a mixture of various alpines a compromise is necessary.

When growers in different regions, gardening in different conditions and using different mixtures, produce equally good results with a particular plant, it has to be accepted that there is no such thing as 'the best soil mixture'. So there is no call for pharmaceutical precision in making up mixtures; there are no magic ingredients, no indispensable materials, but just a few basic requirements to be met.

The most popular use of the raised bed is to grow a collection of plants from a variety of habitats and this calls for a soil mixture that all will find acceptable, even though it will not be the ideal for some. For this the compromise is crude but effective. If the garden is lucky enough to contain fibrous loam with a pH of 6 to 7, it is only necessary to mix this with an equal bulk of gravel or chippings. 'Chippings' is a name used by rock gardeners to cover crushed flint, granite, sandstone and limestone of the grade used by builders in the making of finer concretes, ranging from the size of a sugar lump to a small pea. 'Gravel' is the label for smaller grades going down from pea to sweetener-tablet size. The

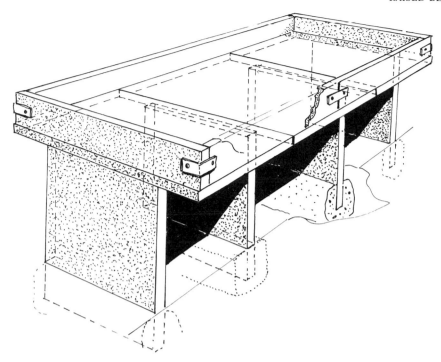

Figure 10 A slab-construction table bed

plants seem indifferent to which of these sizes and types is used, and very few resent limestone, even though they may come from acid soils.

The great majority of gardens do not have fibrous loam to hand and in many cases nothing that even approaches it. Heavy clay soils, and at the other extreme, very sandy soils, are equally unsuitable, the clays being too dense and sticky for the finer roots of many rock plants, and the sands incapable of holding sufficient moisture reserves to sustain the plants even in short dry spells. The sands also lose nutrients rapidly. The average garden soil (if there is such a thing) usually lacks enough fibrous material to retain moisture when it is opened up by the addition of gravel or chippings. In the majority of cases, therefore, it will be necessary to manufacture the 'soil' component of the mixture in the form of a substitute loam.

Sandy soil needs to be enriched with fibrous material and here there is a choice. Peat, composted bark, bracken litter, good garden compost, leaf-mould and spruce needles will all serve the purpose, as will any combination of them. Sawdust should be avoided as it is often very resinous and also takes a long time to break down into useful humus.

Clay soil needs solid material to open up its structure, as well as fibrous material to improve its texture. If one part of clay soil (by volume) is combined with one part grit or coarse sand and one part of any of the organic materials given for sands, it should approach loam in character and behaviour.

Imported soils are chancy; they can be excellent or they may conceal millions of latent weeds waiting for the opportunity to run riot. If these include mares-tail or ground elder then the bed will be a disaster area, requiring a total emptying and refilling.

The foregoing has dealt with the 'half-and-half' mixture for the cosmopolitan bed and with luck, it will be just about right for 30–40 per cent of the inhabitants and acceptable to the remainder. If the bed's population is restricted to a particular type of plant, it is possible to approach the ideal mixture for most of them. A typical example is the scree bed, prepared specifically for plants that are by nature scree dwellers and others needing similar rooting, such as those from crevices and shingle.

A trial excavation into a natural scree, or the examination of one which has been cut through by road works or pipe-laying, will reveal how little organic material is present. The major difference between the real thing and the gardener's imitation is size. Wild plants are spaced well apart and can explore great volumes of debris, whereas those in captivity are very much more limited, living in close proximity and in competition for space, water and food. Here again there is a need for compromise. The open, stony and superbly drained root-run must be provided, but the organic material has to be more plentiful to satisfy the demands of a dense population. As usual, a lot depends on locality and climate when deciding upon proportions and balances.

In Britain, annual rainfall can be up to four times greater in northern and western regions than in those of the south-east. Such rain-gauge comparisons are not conclusive, because also important are how *often* it rains and how the total hours of sunshine compare; nevertheless, there are clearly wet, cool regions, dry, warm regions and all the variations in-between them.

If the locality is of the wetter, cooler type, the amount of moisture-retaining material in the mix will not need to be as high as is necessary in the drier ones. As a result scree mixtures range considerably and perhaps the best guidance that can be given is to present two extreme examples, which have both proved successful for several years. The first is in a cool, wet garden in NW England, with an annual rainfall of 170cm (63in): 3 parts chippings, 1 part leaf-mould and sedge peat mixed. The second is a dry, windy site, near the east coast of Scotland, with an annual rainfall of 58cm (23in): 2 parts chippings, 1 part grit, 2 parts loam and peat mixed.

In the preparation of scree mixtures a little feed material is often incorporated, but only a little. Enough slow-release, low-nitrogen fertiliser to fill a teacup is sufficient for six large barrow loads of the mixture.

At the other extreme is the make-up for an ericaceous planting, which frequently includes woodland species. Good drainage is still important, but it must be in combination with a very high fibre and humus content, forming the spongy texture required. Wherever the bed is built, the same basic properties are required, hence in wetter areas it will merely shed excess water and in dry areas will soak up and hold in reserve the less frequent and lighter rainfall. There is no case here of re-creating something which occurs in a distant place with greatly different seasons and conditions; ericaceous habitats are common in our own landscapes.

Here is an example of a tried and tested mixture which has proved its worth in many gardens, and which may only require a little more drainage material in extremely wet areas. The proportions by volume are: 2 parts leaf-mould, 2 parts sphagnum peat, 1 part coarse, lime-free sand or 3mm ($\frac{1}{8}$in) granite gravel. A trace of plant food is often added, e.g. an egg-cupful of blood, fish and bonemeal to each barrow load.

The raised bed offers an excellent home to bulbous plants and can be devoted to a collection of these with special preparation. Symmetrical beds are easily fitted with a removable glass cover which will give the summer dry-out needed by many species to give of their best. A further use of the cover is to regulate the amount of rain that the bed receives in autumn and winter. The filling material is not too critical, although a fertile and somewhat sandy soil is often recommended as the type to aim for. On the whole, bulbs require much more food than alpines and the soil mixtures should take this into account. A rough guide would be to use a cupful of a balanced, slow-release, low-nitrogen fertiliser to each barrow load of the prepared soil mixture.

For table beds the filling mixtures for raised beds are quite satisfactory, with the exception of the very lean scree mixtures, which would dry out far too rapidly in the elevated, shallow containment. A better scree mix in this case would have the gravel or chippings content reduced by 30–40 per cent.

The mechanics of filling

For small beds, say up to the size of an ordinary dining table, this task does not present any major problems; it can be done by the bucketful or by transferring from barrow to bed with a spade. Larger beds and especially those of appreciable depth, require different techniques. A hired cement mixer is well worth considering for preparing the blend of materials making up the filling mixture. Even so, shovelling load after load of the mixer's product into the bed is a job for the fit, young gardener; for the rest of us there are useful aids. A ramp rising from ground level to the top of the bed wall can be made from a stout plank or two, allowing a barrow to be wheeled up and tipped into the bed. If the ramp is steep, the barrow can be assisted up the slope by a helper pulling on a rope fastened to the front of the barrow. This technique was much used by the 'navvies' employed in the building of our railways and canals.

It is a mistake to deposit all of the required filling mixture into the bed in one operation. It needs progressive consolidation if it is not to settle disastrously in the months following the fill.

When the mixture has been evenly spread in the bed to a spade's depth it should be thoroughly trampled down and any steps or cavities in the wall's inner face should be solidly packed. The same treatment is applied to the next spade's depth of mixture deposited and so on to complete the fill. If this is not

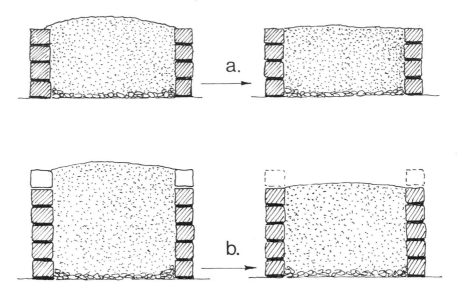

*Figure 11 Compensating for filling settlement **a**. overfilling **b**. temporary top course*

done there will be a marked general settlement plus localised slumping, as time and weather do the job in their own way. In spite of taking these measures, an amount of settlement is unavoidable and as a rough guide, it can be expected that the level of the finished fill will drop by about 4cm (1½in) for each 30cm (12in) of bed depth, over the ensuing year or so. Compensation for this action can be incorporated in the manner of filling, and it is certainly worth doing to avoid the subsequent unattractive look of a bed with a soil surface noticeably below the wall top. There are two techniques, the first being for beds of low to moderate depth. Here the bed is over-filled and cambered to provide an initial surplus of mixture, which will make up the loss to settlement and give a final surface which is still slightly above or level with, the wall top. The second employs a temporary top course of stone, brick or walling block, which is left unmortared and is removed when the fill has settled to a lower level. Figure 11 illustrates the two methods. The techniques and precautions described apply equally to the various mixtures required for scree plants, general alpine collections and ericaceous or woodland types, also to all the different styles and forms of raised beds.

One point of recurrent controversy in bed filling, is the need for a shallow layer of drainage material in the base. The usual form employs small-sized rubble or coarse stone chippings, covered with a blanket of fibrous material, such as turves, with much of their soil knocked off, or 'top-spit' peat containing plenty of roots and twigs. The intended action of the blanket is to prevent soil from working down and clogging the drainage, but giving free passage to water.

There are two arguments in opposition, one being that the filtering blanket merely moves the blockage problem upwards, clogging the filter instead of the

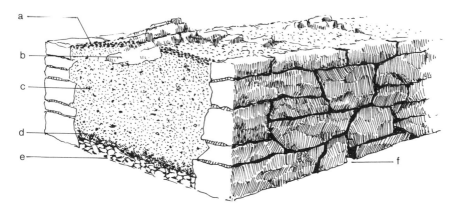

*Figure 12 The anatomy of a raised bed **a**. surface or top dressing **b**. crevice rocks **c**. soil mixture **d**. fibrous filter layer **e**. drainage rubble **f**. drainage outlet*

rubble. The other sees no need for a drainage layer, reasoning that if the soil mixture is adequately porous the water will pass through easily.

No clear winner has emerged; some growers insist that the base drainage is essential and others ignore it. The one thing they all have in common is a beautiful raised bed full of healthy plants!

Surfacing the bed

All the successful surfacings are essentially the same, in that they use stone fragments, in one form or another, to separate the base or neck of the plant from the moister soil mixture, shed water rapidly and ensure a generous circulation of air.

There are additional benefits to be gained by applying this finishing layer. Soil-splash onto foliage and flowers in heavy rain is eliminated. The seeds of many weeds find it difficult to germinate and others that do manage to take root are easily spotted and extracted when young. In dry periods loss of moisture from the bed by evaporation is significantly slowed down due to the mulching effect. The compacting, or 'panning' effect, of heavy downpours on the surface of the soil mixture is greatly reduced.

The choice of surfacing material is influenced by availability and suitability. It is often difficult to find stone chippings or coarse gravel to harmonise with the colour and texture of the bed material and if some rockwork has been added it can increase the problem. Locally available material may be functionally perfect for the purpose but at odds with the structure. For instance, the rounded gravels from pits, rivers or sea-shores just do not blend with angular stones. The rich amber and honey hues of flint chippings are too much for association with the more gentle colours of most sandstones, and completely in conflict with the grey-white limestones. Strong colour in the surfacings can also detract from the flowers grown there, especially those composed of materials

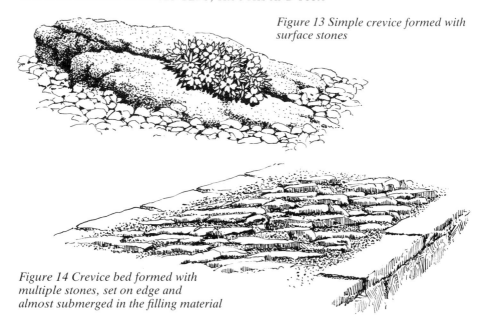

Figure 13 Simple crevice formed with surface stones

Figure 14 Crevice bed formed with multiple stones, set on edge and almost submerged in the filling material

with a pronounced pink or blue cast. At the extreme however, it is better to have a surface, whatever its visual effect, than to leave the filling mixture uncovered, principally for the sake of the plants, but also to protect the bed generally and to minimise maintenance.

A common shortcoming in applying the surfacing, or top dressing as it is often called, is a lack of adequate thickness. Frequently it is merely a garnishing, which looks well but fails in its purpose. To be fully effective the thickness of the layer should be at least 2.5cm (1in) and preferably 5cm (2in). If less it will be quickly invaded by mosses and pearlworts etc., because they can find rooting and sustenance just below the surface. A thin layer also fails to provide the insulation and separation so beneficial to the plants.

Ideally then the bed will bear a blanket of stone chippings, gravel, crushed shale or even shingle, of a generous depth and if at all possible, with some variation in size. Pristine, uniformly sized gravel can have a very funereal look about it.

Rockwork is very often added to a raised bed as simply a few ornamental stones or, at the other extreme, as a principal feature, arranged to form miniature outcrops with ledges and crevices. In either case it is largely an embellishment to the looks of a bed but it does create opportunities for crevice planting. Normally this form of planting is associated with walls and elaborate rockwork, yet it often fails in these places, the plants becoming dislodged by weather action or shrivelled by lack of water, being unable to root quickly and deeply enough to combat these ills. A crevice can be contrived by the close positioning of stones on the surface of the raised bed (Figures 13 and 14). Using this arrangement the stones need not be monumental in size yet they form an

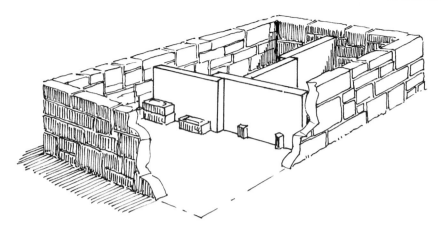

Figure 15 Bed compartments

attractive crevice with a stable and well-prepared root-run beneath it, offering far greater hope of success to anything planted in it.

Planting schemes

It has already been recognised that beds can be tailored for particular plant types or collections. In addition they can be designed or adapted for other specific plantings, such as:

Geographical   Where the plants are all native to a particular region, country or continent.

Successional   Involving careful selection and positioning of plants to ensure a sequence of flowers through the seasons.

Landscaped   Creating a miniature terrain, incorporating a variety of habitats with picturesque effect.

In order to support a representative collection of plants, the geographical bed may need to provide several aspects and soil mixtures. This means that it will have to be of sufficient size to accommodate these. It is quite feasible to physically divide the bed into compartments for differing soil mixtures by the use of paving slabs. The slabs are set up within the bed and held upright by wooden pegs or stones at the base. There is no need for more elaborate support because the filling material will do this job if the compartments are filled simultaneously (in this way the levels rise at roughly the same rate). The slabs should be sized to have their top edges just below the finished wall height so that they are eventually submerged and invisible (Figure 15). This method is valid for other plantings where similar segregation is required. Unless they are of a great size and created with professional skill and funding, map-shaped beds with appropriately planted regions are too ambitious for the amateur's garden (and pocket) and invariably fail. It is much more practical to concentrate on a section of the flora and create a habitat that is as near to the ideal as possible.

Successional plantings need a lot of preparatory work in the armchair before they can be put into action. A lot of ideas have to be tested against practicalities and there is much trial and error before a reliable plan begins to emerge. The aim is to avoid having areas that are colourful and interesting for only a week or two and drab or featureless for the remainder of the year. In achieving this, plant selection is strongly influenced by the time of flowering, but there are other considerations too. Having decided that a mat-forming plant, flowering in early summer, could be underplanted with spring bulbs to give earlier colour, the planner has then to find companion plants to give flowers later in the year, but when these have been carefully chosen, the job is by no means complete; the selected plants have then to be vetted for living together. Do they all enjoy full sun or do one or two require some shade? Will the same soil mixture be acceptable to all of them? Is the mat-former going to be too vigorous in growth and a threat to its neighbours? Will the spot be dry enough for the bulbs without parching the other plants? These are typical of the questions that must be asked if the final result is to be a success.

Landscaped beds hold a fascination for many growers of alpine plants. Miniature outcrops are usually the main features, supported by dwarf trees, minutely leaved carpeting plants and tiny flowering shrubs. It is impossible to hold all these to a true scale but the general effect can be very eye-catching. Very careful selection of plants is essential to avoid 'rogues' spoiling the balance and scale of the matured planting.

Even with such care there will inevitably be the odd species that outgrows its allotted space and another that simply refuses to flourish, leaving a bald spot in the landscape. Nevertheless, the planning and creation of these 'Tom Thumb' gardens can be absorbing and great fun for the artistically inclined.

Because a relatively small amount of rock is involved and the individual pieces are easily handled, it is worth while seeking out really attractive weathered stones for the scaled-down outcrops and boulders. Similar care in the choice of surfacing chippings or gravel is well repaid in the resulting appearance of the finished bed. A sceptical eye should be cast on catalogue lists of 'dwarf' trees and shrubs suitable for such plantings. Very few are truly dwarf, or remain so beyond a few years of residence. Specialist nurseries are the safer source of advice and plants for what are, after all, long-term, important features.

Practicalities of planting

Some of the infant mortality rate among rock plants is probably due to faulty planting at the outset. The victims never really had a fair chance, being handicapped from their first day in the garden.

There are several ways in which planting can be badly done and perhaps the most common of these is born of a misunderstanding.(It is assumed, by the way, that the plant has been received, or has been home-grown, in a small nursery pot and is apparently in good health at the time of planting.) This misunderstanding is that the whole operation should be carried out with the absolute minimum of disturbance to the root ball. To this end great pains are taken to ease the plant from its pot and to gently transfer it to the prepared hole in the bed. Once there the soil mixture is carefully and lightly packed around the root ball and surface chippings are smoothed up to the neck of the plant. The flaw in all this commendable care is that the roots are almost invariably congested within the pot. They have encircled the confined space many times, interweaving and tangling in their search for moisture and food. Left in this state they are very slow to explore their new surroundings and in dry periods it is quite possible for the whole root ball to parch whilst surrounded by still-moist material. Similarly, the need for fresh nutrients, to sustain new growth and development, is poorly served by the closely compacted mass of root. The result can be death due to drought, despite attention given to watering the bed, or a plant failing to 'pick up', making no fresh foliage, blooming sparsely or not at all and at worst, dying back and becoming easy prey to diseases and pests.

This unhappy state of affairs can be avoided to a large extent by adopting methods that appear brutal yet greatly increase the chances for the juvenile plant. Having made sure that the soil ball is reasonably moist but not sodden, the plant is knocked out of its pot and then as much as possible of the growing medium should be shaken, probed and teased away from the roots. Some skilled growers start this process by dropping the whole thing onto the potting bench from chest height then bounce the remaining root ball in a cupped hand. However it is achieved, the aim is to free the entangled roots so that they may be drawn out to their full length. Obviously it is a task that should not be done in direct sun or in very drying conditions, otherwise permanent damage will be done to the finer roots and root hairs.

Prior to liberating the root system the planting hole should be prepared, erring on the generous side in size, for it must take the freely spread roots comfortably. It is not necessary to make the depth equal to the longest of the roots, as in many cases this would be impractical. A full trowel depth should be adequate for any young plant. With the excavated soil mix piled adjacent to the hole, the root system is spread evenly, with the plant held by its neck at the finished surface level. With this hold on the plant maintained, the soil mixture is then returned to the hole in handfuls until the roots are covered. A gentle firming is then applied and further mixture added until it meets the surrounding level. The final phase is to bring surfacing material up to the natural base of the plant and this is best done by working from the centre of the plant outwards. The chippings, gravel etc. can then be worked up to the stem first, thus making sure that the most important area is thoroughly covered.

In very open mixtures such as those prepared for scree beds, the planting hole often has to be made larger than the root spread to be catered for, to compensate for the material tumbling back into the hole.

Sadly, many nurseries now use peat-based composts for growing rock plants. Such composts aggravate the problem of weaning the bought plant from pot to garden. This only strengthens the argument for baring the roots before planting. If a plant grown in this medium is transferred, undisturbed, to the stony soil of an alpine bed, the difference in texture and behaviour of the two substances is considerable. As a result the plant may never venture into the leaner, but more natural root-run offered by the bed and after exhausting any sustenance remaining in the root ball it will rapidly decline. Another benefit from root freeing is that any soil pests such as vine weevil larvae or cut-worms are likely to be exposed and a potential problem can be immediately eliminated.

Timing can also influence the results of planting. A mild spell in January might seem to be an ideal opportunity to introduce a batch of plants to their garden bed. They are likely to have been acquired over the late weeks of the previous year, from catalogue orders and nursery visits and are standing around in their pots looking vulnerable. Once planted they appear safer, but this is a false impression, for the winter weather can change dramatically. A hard frost following the gentler period has the power to heave the unestablished plants partially or even completely out of the ground. Biting winds, especially those from the east, are very dehydrating and the newly introduced plant is less able to make up the water loss because its root system is immature and still recovering from the shock of transplanting. It is far safer to keep the new plants in their nursery pots in a protected place such as a greenhouse or frame until there are definite signs of spring, when they can be moved into the garden with far less risk.

At the other extreme, summer planting can carry equal perils, again principally associated with dehydration, but in this case caused by sun and dry, warm air. This leaves spring and autumn as the times of least risk and much has been argued on the merits of these two seasons as the better time for planting. There is no clear-cut reasoning for preferring one over the other as a lot depends on the behaviour of individual plants involved. A species that makes a very early start into growth and flower may benefit from autumn planting, in that it will have a few weeks to recover before winter sets in, whereas a spring planting will give it shock and distress at the very time when it should be vigorously developing. For those that waken later, spring planting has its advantages; conditions are steadily improving, encouraging growth and establishment, and there are several months ahead for the plant to actively secure its position, and adjust to the new environment before it experiences adverse weather.

Set apart from these reasonings are the bulbs. Many are dormant through the summer months and are planted in that period. In spring and autumn they are active in some way and will suffer from disturbance, in some cases to a fatal extent.

Crevice planting involves quite different techniques and these vary also with the type of crevice. The very simple arrangement contrived with adjacent stones laid on the surface of the bed (Figure 13) requires only a modification to the method already described for general planting. The hole is scooped out, the

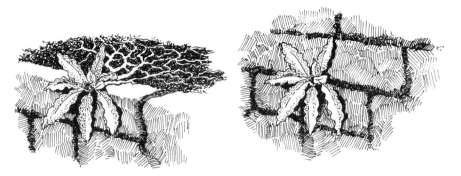

Figure 16 Crevice planting during wall building

roots are spread out within it and the filling is gently returned until it is at a level to form a seating for the stones. These are then positioned either side of the plant as closely together as is possible without damaging the stems or neck, and then stabilised by bringing surface chippings up to them. Fingers are the best tools for pushing the chippings under the stones and between them to achieve a firmness and lack of cavities in the finished work.

The planting of wall crevices requires preparation and skill and has to be done thoroughly if it is to have a good chance of succeeding. Scraping out a joint in an existing wall, tamping the plant's root system into it and packing with a wad of coarse peat or clay is a recipe for failure. Alternating dry and wet periods, frost and rainwater run-off will all act to loosen and dislodge the packing and without it the plant quickly loses its anchorage. The surest method is to incorporate planting in the building of the bed, or in the case of an existing wall, dismantling a section to create the same situation. It requires an alteration to the manner in which the bed is built; instead of completing the structure first and then putting in the filling mixture, these two operations proceed together, in stages. When the lower courses have been laid and secured, filling mixture is introduced and firmed until it is level with the top of the partly completed wall. Plants can then be placed at selected spots with their roots spread out over the surface of the filling mixture (Figure 16). Coarse peat fibres or other similar wadding is placed beneath and over the roots where they lie across the wall surface, together with one or two pebbles. These act as cushioning and chocks for the overlying stone of subsequent courses, preventing crushing of the roots and the crown of the plant. By such means the plant is given immediate firm anchorage and excellent contact between the roots and the growing medium.

When adding further courses above the planted level the mortar should be laid right up to the cushioning collar described above, otherwise the effects of weather will loosen the packing and the plant will lose its firm holding. Even better security is achieved if the final trowelling of the mortar runs a thin layer over much of the exposed cushioning collar and almost touches the plant. This will make certain that the packing stays in place and if the plant subsequently

41

thickens its neck, as it becomes larger, the thin mortar will easily crack away under the pressure without any harm to the growing tissue.

As building and filling progresses, further plantings can be made in the same way and at various levels in the wall. Species that cascade from rock ledges in nature, or crevice plants producing arching plumes of flower, are at their best in such wall plantings. Cushion plants and others vulnerable to winter rotting fare much better on the vertical wall faces, where no excess moisture can linger to do its damage.

Aftercare

The considerable disturbance suffered by the root system in the planting method recommended does inflict some damage. The finer roots and the all-important root hairs are the parts mainly affected and they need time to recover. Whilst they are doing so their ability to supply the plant with water and nutrients is diminished. If during this recovery time the weather provides regular rainfall and no drying winds, the only help needed by the plant is shading, if the sun comes out strongly from time to time. In drier conditions, shading, a windbreak and regular attention to watering are the ways in which the gardener can aid the plant. This is not so time-consuming and bothersome as it may seem. Shading and/or wind protection can both be provided by the same means, a piece of slate, or similar material, propped over the plant and held secure by stones or pegs.

Watering is simply a routine and in the free-draining mixtures used for alpine root-runs it can be applied daily without causing excessive wetness, so there is no need for frequent inspections to ascertain whether or not water should be supplied. After three or four weeks the new plant should be sufficiently recovered to do without the special care and fend for itself. A weekly check on its health for a further month should be all that is needed, mainly to look for signs of pests or diseases. In the case of the most voracious pest, the slug, it should be assumed that this is lying in wait for the tender new plant on the very first day and poison bait must be laid down in anticipation, but beware of endangering harmless slug-eaters. (see p.**123**)

If new plants have been introduced to the bed in the late year, they can be quite violently disturbed by the action of frosts before they have had time to get a firm root-hold. This danger is greatest where the soil mixture has a high proportion of moisture-retaining material, such as peat, bark or leaf-mould. When the stored moisture freezes it expands and lifts the upper inch or two of the soil mixture. Plants that have not developed strong anchoring roots, rise with the frozen crust, but do not sink back with it when the ground thaws. A few repeats of this cycle, typical of night-time freezing and day-time melt, can progressively jack the plant out of the soil. It is often recommended that to combat the effect, a patrol should be made after each frost and the casualties pushed back into the earth, but this can badly damage the exposed roots, An effective and safer alternative, requiring much less time and attention, is to ring the vulnerable plants with small flat stones, their inside ends pushed close to the crown or stem. It is their insulating effect and not their weight that greatly reduces the action of frost and they can be left in place for the whole winter to do their job. Lighter insulating materials would work equally well, but they are all too often blown away or shifted by foraging birds.

So far the aftercare has been applied to individual plants, but it could be that an entire bed, or a large area of one, has been newly planted and all of the young population are needful of attention. Modern materials provide the means for this group protection, in the form of loosely woven plastic strands or very fine mesh. Both give first-class protection against wind and are also excellent for creating finely broken shade. Simple wooden frames are all that is needed to carry an expanse of the material and these can be supported on a few bricks with one or two used as hold-down weights. Nothing more elaborate is necessary because these devices are only for a short-term use, so their crudeness and detraction in the appearance of the bed are of no great matter. An even simpler approach is to tap in a number of wooden pegs around the edges of the bed and along its centre. The same materials as before can then be draped over the bed and adjusted to give headroom for the plants. Rainfall and watering are unimpeded, passing easily through the mesh, but feathered and furred vandals are denied access.

Weather protection

To the general gardener it can seem strange that plants capable of combating the harsh climates of the high mountains should need any protection from the weather. The need stems from the difference in the weather prevailing in our lowland gardens and that of the altitudes, particularly in the months when the plants lie dormant. Wetness, even in small amounts, is quite alien to the sleeping alpine plant; it is accustomed either to a deep covering of crisp, dry snow, or to exposed places where it is too cold for rain to fall.

In either case the plant has never needed to develop a resistance to being saturated for days at a time when it is at a low ebb. In our relatively mild winters fungal diseases can still flourish and they do this best where damp conditions are sustained for long periods. If the plants can be protected against this state, then much has been done to discourage attack by fungi, and the chances of winter survival are considerably improved. For most of the alpine species it does not seem to matter that their root-run is frequently wetted as long as the foliage or resting buds are sheltered from the rain, which confirms that it is the above-ground parts of the plant that are the most susceptible to fungal diseases.

Whatever device is used to give overhead shelter from the rain it must have two essential features: transparency and ventilation. If the material precludes too much light the plant beneath will become drawn and pallid, because in cultivation it is not truly dormant and so still needs this element. If the protection is too enclosed it will create a dank micro-climate around the plant, and far from being discouraged, fungal diseases will thrive.

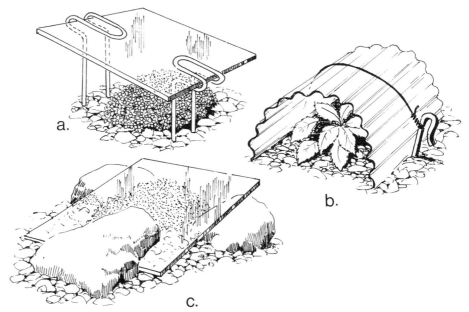

*Figure 17 Individual plant covers **a**. glass with wire clips **b**. corrugated plastic with guy wire **c**. glass and stones*

For a single plant of modest spread nothing has yet been devised to better the small pane of glass (or transparent plastic) to act as a winter umbrella. It meets the two essentials just described and is simple, cheap and easily replaced if broken or blown away. There are several ways, however, of fixing this little roof in place and these warrant some comment.

Ingeniously bent wires in a variety of shapes have been developed to do the twofold task of gripping and holding down (Figure 17.a). Their greatest merit is that they take up virtually no ground space, but they lack real tenacity when the wind blows strongly, the thin legs being uprooted by the tugging of the cover.

Another form employs a corrugated plastic sheet bent into a half-tube and anchored by a wire and pegs (Figure 17.b). This makes a very firm and serviceable cover with no vices, although its bottom edges may encroach on nearby plants or be difficult to juggle around rocks in the vicinity. The simplest arrangement (Figure 17.c) works well, but does take up ground space; it uses only stones to position and secure the cover. All of these artefacts allow abundant circulation of air, keeping the harmful dankness at bay.

For groups of plants, or indeed a whole bed, the small makeshift shelter principles are inadequate and a better engineered covering is needed if it is to function reliably and stay in place. Rectangular beds can often be effectively protected by using the conventional frame light. If it is large enough to span the walls of the bed then it is only necessary to add supports under one end to produce the slope needed to shed rainwater away from the bed. One or two bricks will do this job perfectly well, but there must also be sound securement

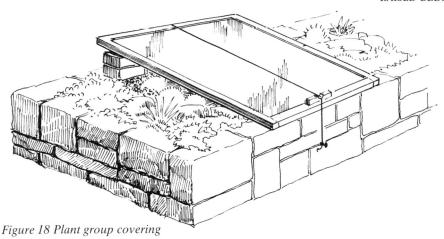

Figure 18 Plant group covering

against winds. Figure 18 shows a typical arrangement with a securing guy fastened to stout nails housed in close-fitting holes drilled into mortar joints. Soft stretchy rope is unsuitable for the guy as it will allow the cover to bounce in windy weather, progressively loosening the securement. Strong coated wire, of the type used to train wall plants, has the strength and rigidity required and should be drawn taut when fixed in place. Covers of a similar pattern can be tailor-made to suit a bed, using very simple wooden frames covered with heavy-gauge plastic. The latter must be well fixed to the framework, a good method being to use wooden strips tacked to the outside edges, over the plastic sheet (Figure 19).

Informally shaped beds pose problems for group or overall coverage. Tailored covers involve strange geometries with complex securing difficulties. The way out of these troubles is to design round them in the planting scheme, putting those species vulnerable to winter wet in colonies, over which a simple covering frame can be placed. This does not mean that the selected plants will be in a rectangular huddle; they will merely be confined to an area that can be accommodated under the sheltering cover. If the area includes a rock or two and some plants that do not need the protection, it matters little (Figure 20).

From such extended shelters it is a natural progression to the all-over roof, which may be temporary or permanent. The temporary version is usually a light, easily handled structure put up in the autumn and dismantled when spring growth starts. Few gardeners favour this yearly up and down chore with the attendant storage problems, and where total coverage is employed it is usually permanent once erected. Even so an option remains, which is to have or not to have permanent *covering* on the structure and here there is no favourite. It is perhaps helpful to explain that the structure will probably look something like a pergola under which sits the bed, or it might be in the form of a veranda along a house wall. Either type must be tall enough to walk under and they are illustrated in Figure 21. In both types, the covering material (glass or plastic) can be permanent or designed for seasonal removal and replacement.

45

These are expensive facilities and whilst they are airy and light their height allows much more wind-blown rain to reach the plants in winter squalls. It could be said that such structures are little different from an alpine house, the latter just having some side glazing added, but this strays beyond the subjects and limits of this book.

The best that can be done for an entire bed is probably to incorporate at the building stage, locations and anchorage points for a set of frame lights. Here there is a chicken-and-egg situation, for either the bed dimensions are made to suit a particular size of light, or a set of lights is made to suit the bed dimensions. The decision may be easy if a set of lights is available. Where the bed already exists and is not sized to standard frame dimensions it pays to reject inclinations to 'make do' with bits and pieces and to build or acquire well-fitting covers. Old house windows, large picture frames and left-overs from the old greenhouse are never satisfactory. In addition to being an eyesore they attract a motley collection of hold-down fastenings and supports, invariably let drips through in places — and of course over the most prized plants!

Watering

Amongst newcomers to the cultivation of rock-garden plants and those who are in the earlier stages of acquiring experience, one of the major uncertainties is with regard to watering. There are many warnings about the dire results of over- or under-watering, but little in the way of clear guidance. This is not due to a reluctance amongst skilled growers to pass on valuable information, it is just that they don't have precise instruction to offer.

Their skill and understanding has been acquired from years of work, with a lot of trial and error, leading to the development of a 'feel' for when water is needed. This may seem fanciful but the 'feel' is really a response to a number of observations that the grower makes without consciously doing so. Certain plants give early signals of failing moisture supplies and these may be quite subtle; just a loss of sheen to the leaf or a slight arching of normally upright

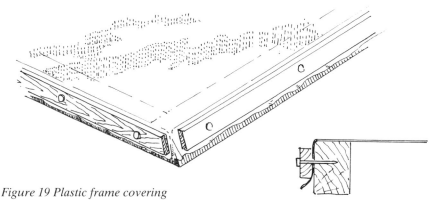

Figure 19 Plastic frame covering

Figure 20 Localised covering for informal bed

stems, a hint of laxness in the packed rosettes of a cushion plant, or a dulling of flower colour.

Only long experience and familiarity with the plants can bestow such expertise, but there are one or two things that the less-experienced gardener can do to gauge the need for water. Keeping a simple daily record of the local weather is useful in several ways, one of which is knowing exactly when rain last fell; reliance on memory is often wildly inaccurate. This information, coupled with a knowledge of how quickly the bed dries out, provides a guide for the need to water. The bed's drying-out rate can be established by periodically exposing the soil mixture beneath the top dressing and judging its moistness. If it takes seven to eight days of rain-free, sunny weather to dry out the top inch or so of the soil mixture, then there is no need to water until such a period has elapsed (after significant rain). This simple measure takes account of local conditions and the particular soil mixture concerned, because the tests have been made on the spot. If all that seems too complicated, then the moisture check can be made every other day during a dry spell and watering commenced only when the surface of the soil beneath the top dressing is visibly dry.

The approach of 'if in doubt: water' can do more harm than good. A *little* drying-out persuades the plants to root deeper for their moisture supplies, giving them more stamina when drought does hit them. On the other hand, if they are always watered at the slightest hint of drying they never make such reinforcements. As a result they suffer parching earlier if the weather sets fair and the waterer is not there to give them their regular dose.

The drying rate of a bed depends to a large extent on the nature of the filling mixture. The very aerated scree compounds are the first to reach danger level, whilst the fibre-rich woodland or ericaceous beds hold their moisture far longer. Again, it is a matter of testing to establish just how long a particular bed can go without rainfall before the gardener must intervene and make good the loss. At the very extreme, although with some risk of causing drought damage to one or two plants, it could be said that there is no need to water until

47

something wilts. Although such treatment is harsh, a trial based on this distress-signal system will surprise many growers as to how long watering can be deferred until it is absolutely necessary.

When water is supplied artificially, by whatever system is employed, i.e. can, hose, sprinkler etc. it must be done copiously. The evening potter round the beds to give each plant a brief douche from the watering can, is nothing like enough to restore the moisture balance. The truth is easily confirmed by watering a plant in this fashion and then scraping away the surface of the wetted area. It is unlikely that the water will have penetrated much below the top dressing, which leaves it a long way above the needy roots.

To avoid disturbing the bed's surface or causing 'flood damage' the water should fall onto it rather than be sprayed at it. This requires some form of sprinkler head on a hose to throw droplets into the air for a gentle descent onto the bed. Using such equipment can give a false impression of the amount of water that is being delivered. After ten minutes or so the bed may appear to be thoroughly drenched, but in fact is only superficially wetted, lacking adequate penetration. A flat-bottomed dish placed on the bed just before watering begins will indicate, on the rain-gauge principle, just how much water has fallen. Until the depth of water collected approaches 12mm ($\frac{1}{2}$in) it is unlikely that the bed has been fully saturated. If a check is made on the time taken to achieve sufficient water depth it can be used as a guide for future waterings.

When a bed has been soaked in this manner the moisture levels are fully restored and it can be regarded as having been rained upon for a day or so. Accordingly, it will sustain its occupants for several days of dry weather before the same treatment is required again.

The foregoing applies to beds with established populations. Where newly introduced plants are present, these must be given individual attention and will require watering far more frequently. In dry weather a generous application every day is not excessive, giving each plant at least half a litre (1 pint).

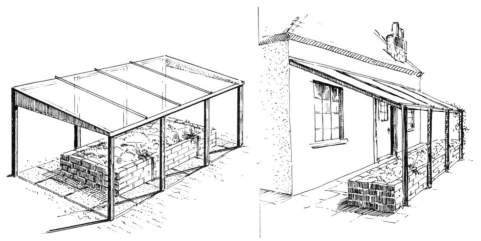

Figure 21 Covered raised beds in 'pergola' and 'veranda' forms

Bewildering arrays of watering devices confront us nowadays, in garden centres, hardware shops and stores, with varying degrees of technology incorporated in them. It may be cynical but probably true to say that the more complex the system the more likely it is to go wrong, particularly in the absence of the gardener. In principle the systems fall into four basic categories. Fixed sprays, which deliver multiple fine jets of water, something like an amplified watering-can rose. (Some are static whilst others gyrate or oscillate to increase the area wetted.) Adjustable sprays, where a nozzle can be 'tuned' to give a variety of droplet sizes and spray patterns. Atomisers, which produce very fine droplet sizes and give a very gentle 'drizzle' effect. Perforated hoses, of two types, one sending up little fountains at regular intervals, the other dribbling onto the ground.

None of these can be picked out as superior for the purpose of watering raised beds, their suitability and effectiveness depend to a great extent on the size, shape and architecture of the garden and its beds.

Permanently installed watering systems are efficient, labour-saving and expensive. Also, unless they are cleverly concealed, they can be intrusive and something of an eyesore. Nevertheless, in the larger gardens they certainly warrant consideration and they can be unobtrusive as some of the public gardens have demonstrated. Recent developments have produced impulse jets which are barely above ground level yet cover an amazingly large area with their tiny oscillating water cannons.

The other form of fixed installation, beloved of Victorian rock gardeners, is the subterranean system, where perforated pipes are laid down in the making of the bed. A trickle feed maintains a steady seepage of water at lower levels in the bed. These are mainly associated with scree gardens where the water is unable to stagnate or over-saturate the root-run. Their main drawback is in being invisible, so that their performance and condition can only be guessed at and they do become blocked, through sediment, corrosion and algae growths.

Coming back to the surface again, there is a warning found in many sources of cultivation lore that watering should never be carried out on a sunny day. The consequence, we are told, is scorching of foliage due to water droplets acting as lenses, focusing the suns rays. If this were true, wild alpine plants would be pock-marked with a host of burns, as they are frequently refreshed by a passing shower during otherwise hot sunny days. A more credible reason for avoiding waterings at such times is that some of the liquid will be lost to evaporation before it can benefit the plant, hence the custom of evening watering. If a plant is needing water then it is better given it whilst the sun is shining than left to broil until the evening.

Not every gardener is lucky enough to have good neighbours willing to take care of the watering during a holiday or other such lengthy absence, in which case an automated watering system can solve worrying problems. The least complicated of the systems is probably the one that activates a simple sprinkler arrangement for a fixed length of time each day. A timer is connected to an electrically operated on-off valve in the water supply and at a selected time the valve opens to feed the watering system and closes after a set period of operation. The shortcoming of the principle involved is that the system operates irrespective of the weather, so that the sprinkler will come on even though it may be pouring down at the time. This superfluous watering is not detrimental to the plants, however, as it merely intensifies the rainfall and a properly drained bed will easily cope with the extra-heavy shower.

At far greater expense, automatic systems can be had that use solar sensors to control the watering arrangements. The sensors signal the switch-on only after a certain amount of sunlight has been received and measured since the previous watering. This leaves it to the gardener to decide how much sunshine the plants can take before they need a drink. The alternative technology uses an electrical moisture-meter buried in the soil as the source of its control. Again the dryness at which the system is triggered is adjustable and the onus is on the user to set the limit.

Winter watering of the garden is rarely necessary in this country, but in the interim between winter and true spring there can be times when watering may be called for. These occasions arise when cold easterly winds persist. The winds are by nature dry and searching, taking up moisture from both the soil and the foliage of plants. Dehydration can be brought about by such conditions just as it can be by drought and it may be necessary to resort to watering if plants show distress. Where beds are extensively protected by winter covers there is always a slow but steady drying-out during winter and it is easily overlooked. Every three or four weeks a quick check should be made and water given where necessary, but in moderate amounts, just enough to moisten the soil rather than soak it. For smaller areas such as under a single frame light or individual plant cover, such precaution is unnecessary as moisture will soak in from the unprotected soil surrounding them.

Feeding

In the treatment of bed filling, initial provision of fertiliser was included. For the first year or two after completion and planting of the bed this initial feed, coupled with the freshness of the soil mixture, should be quite sufficient to sustain the needs of the plants. Eventually though, it will be necessary to begin adding feeding substances to compensate for the take-up by the plants and losses due to the leaching action of rain. It is difficult to be precise about when supplements are needed, for as in other matters, it depends upon the local climate and the type and size of the bed. Another factor is the density of planting; a crowded bed will exhaust the food supplies far quicker than one that is only sparsely planted.

Scree beds are likely to need the earliest attention; their open structure hardly hinders the washing out of nutrients by rain, and the high oxygen levels accelerate the break down of beneficial compounds in the 'soil' content of the mixture. By comparison humus-rich, fibrous soils, suiting ericaceous and woodland plants, lose their nutrients less rapidly.

From general experience it is probable that a bed containing a varied collection of alpines will require feeding in the third spring of its existence and each spring from then on. Those with richer fillings may well go at least four years before any attention is required. There are usually some signs of the need to supply sustenance. The more vigorous plants slow down in growth and can begin to look dowdy. Progressive yellowing of leaves can be an indicator, although this is also a symptom for a whole list of plant ailments. A decline in the wealth and quality of flowering is a reliable sign that food is running short.

The manner of feeding depends upon the form used. Powdered or granulated fertilisers are simply scattered over the surface of the bed (avoiding the plants) and left to be washed in by rainfall or watering. Liquid feeds usually require some measured dilution with water before application and are then delivered by watering-can. (Some benefit the plants by being allowed to wet the foliage, others may cause damage.) Foliar feeds are also liquid but usually applied by spray.

Many rock gardeners prefer the dry fertilisers, chiefly because they can be obtained in the slow-release form and hence need only be applied once per year. Liquid feeds are quickly exhausted and require regular, periodic application.

In the earlier exploration of natural alpine habitats, mention was made of the low nitrogen levels in mountain soils and the richness of other elements such as potash. It follows that the fertiliser used should at least have something approaching the same balance of constituents, and the nearest, in commercial compounds, are those intended for promoting the growth of fruit and flower. In the long-established types the 'blood, fish and bone' mixtures are quite suitable. Modern slow-release fertilisers include special preparations with lower nitrogen content and good levels of potash and phosphate, usually packaged as 'rose fertiliser' or 'fruit and flower compound'. These produce satisfactory results and are easy to apply. General fertilisers are invariably too high in nitrogen.

Few alpines have the appetites of plants like herbaceous perennials and food should be given sparingly. Excess will cause them to produce foliage at the expense of flower and can, in some cases, make them more prone to disease. An adequate annual feed for a bed is no more than a light dusting of the surface. This represents about enough to fill an egg-cup evenly scattered over a square metre (ounces, grammes etc. are deliberately avoided, as it is generally much easier to use a familiar volume when out in the garden). There is no need to disturb the surface dressing in order to fork in the fertiliser; rain or watering will quickly wash it in and take the dissolved nutrients down to the roots. This measure of feed seems to be adequate for all the types of bed discussed, with the exception of those dedicated to bulbs; here there is a need for three or four times the amount per square metre to maintain adequate growth and flowering. In applying any dry fertiliser it is always safest to assume that if some should fall onto the leaves of the plant it could be harmful and is better swilled off immediately, or better still, kept off by careful handling initially.

Foliar feeds have been developed and promoted over the last few years and unfortunately, appliances are now available which can easily encourage excesses. Feed solutions are entrained in the watering hose flow and as a result everything that is wetted is also fed, irrespective of its need or whether it is capable of taking in nutrients through its foliage. This form of feeding could be detrimental; there is good evidence confirming that certain alpine plants can be injured by foliar feeds. By comparison dry feeds can be applied more accurately and easily and their effect is long-lasting.

Liquid feeds (watered onto the soil and not the plant) are useful as short-term 'boosters'. A typical example is their regular application to bulbous plants during and for some time after, flowering, a practice common amongst experienced growers with many bulbs in their collections. In the same way liquid feed can improve the flowering of certain alpine plants, such as gentians, where they are known to have an unusually large appetite at the height of their activity. In both cases the quick-acting, but briefly effective liquid is a supplement to the steady output provided by the slow-release food sources applied each spring. Generally speaking, rock gardeners dilute liquid feeds to half the strength specified for other garden plants, and of course use only those with the lower nitrogen content.

Maintenance

Inevitably some plants will fail to prosper for known or unknown reasons. Others will meet their natural demise after several years. Either way their passing leaves an empty place in the planting, offering a home for a new tenant. Removal of the remains warrants some consideration, beyond giving the corpse a hearty tug or delving under it with a trowel. There are species that send out tough, searching roots for quite a distance and if pulled, are likely to heave up a large patch of soil and with it anything else that is growing there. To avoid a major excavation and the disruption of neighbouring plants, the crown and a little of the rootage can be exposed by scraping away the adjacent top dressing and soil to allow severing of the roots at their source. Unlike tree roots their remaining presence in the soil is quite benign as they do not seem to attract harmful fungus in their gradual decay. It is important, however, to revitalise the spot before introducing a replacement. To this end it is only necessary to remove as much of the spent soil mixture as is practicable and to replace it with fresh mixture. This operation is confined to the immediate area where the deceased plant was growing and usually produces no more than half a bucketful for replacement.

Obviously there are many species with modest or delicate root systems which can be uprooted with negligible disturbance. Again it is unnecessary to attempt extensive root removal, but it pays to refresh the soil mixture locally, as already described.

The replacement of crevice plants is quite another matter. Where a plant was originally installed in a wall crevice during the building stage it is not too difficult to remove the remains, but the replanting presents severe problems. True, a hole can be gouged out and the roots of a young plant teased into it, but then soil has to be introduced to gently but firmly pack the roots and it has to stay in place! This resurrects the difficulties described earlier in the section devoted to planting. By painstakingly tamping soil mixture into the crevice and sealing this in with a thin skim of mortar, it is possible to achieve good and lasting results, but it does require careful work and much patience. A less demanding alternative is to repack the crevice and apply retaining mortar to leave just a small entrance. Seed of desired occupant is then inserted and with a measure of good fortune one may germinate and secure an adequate root-hold before it is washed out by seepage or withered by wind and sun. It is chancy, but worth trying and repeating once or twice if first attempts fail.

After a few years, usually between six and eight, even the best prepared bed begins to decline; its plants no longer display the healthy vigour and willingness to bloom that they did in previous years. Fortunately this 'fatigue' rarely afflicts the whole bed at once, but starts here and there in definite patches. Within these many of the plants develop a tired or threadbare appearance despite attention to feeding, watering and protection from pests. The remedy is to thoroughly revitalise the rooting medium, which entails careful lifting and temporary housing of the plants to allow extensive removal and renewal of the soil mixture. The need for this refurbishment is brought about by the alteration of the soil structure with the passage of time and the effects of weather. As the organic constituent is used up there is a loss of water-retaining material and a decline in the multitude of air spaces and waterways due to compaction and the workings of earthworms. Important trace elements are leached out by repeated rainfall and there are changes in the presence of beneficial micro-organisms. All these factors contribute to a loss of vitality and balance in the substance provided for the plants to root in and from which they extract what they need.

The wholesale renewal of an entire bed can be a daunting proposition, as well as presenting grave problems in terms of salvaging as many as possible of the plants growing in it. The patchiness of the decline averts the need for such a major operation, allowing the task to be done in stages as the need arises. It brings the plant handling down to manageable proportions and the physical work to an acceptable level.

Over the area affected the top dressing is removed and discarded, then the soil mixture is also removed. The depth to which this excavation should go depends somewhat on the nature of the bed. A trowel's depth is quite enough for the fibrous mixtures used in ericaceous plantings, as these are mainly inhabited by plants with shallow root systems. At the other extreme a scree bed will require renewal to about the full depth of a spade and this is not an easy task, due to the constant tumbling of the stony mixture into the hole being dug. There is no easy answer to this problem but there are two things that can be done to help matters. The first is to choose a day when the ground is moist rather than on the dry side, which helps the mixture to cling a little, and the second is to do the job slowly and gently, with a trowel, making the least disturbance.

Prior to this digging-out operation there is the work of salvaging some of the plants. This calls for some hard decisions. Mature tap-rooted plants rarely survive transplanting and are best regarded as expendable. The same applies to quite a number of scree-dwelling plants which send down vigorous thongs of root. On the other hand it is worth while taking some trouble to rescue the plants with fibrous root systems, as these can often be coaxed back into healthy growth and many more years of life. If the refurbishing work is to be completed in a day or so then it is only necessary to carefully lift the plant with as much root as possible and put it in a shady place with moist peat over its roots. For a longer absence from the bed the plants are safer if potted in containers, using a 50/50 mixture of peat and grit and protected from strong sunshine and drying winds. Plastic buckets, washing-up bowls and well-cleaned paint containers serve well as temporary homes for the mature plants.

The replacement mixture for the bed repair should be similar in quality and texture to the original bed-filling material. The quantity required is easily judged against the volume taken out. Refilling and replanting go side by side, the salvaged plants, together with new introductions, being positioned and firmed as the soil mixture is replaced. In this manner it is easy to ensure good spreading of the root systems and careful packing of the rooting medium around them. The work is completed by laying fresh top dressing over the surface and under the plants.

Compared with the renovating of a whole bed in a single operation, the stage-by-stage approach has several attractions. Only certain areas of the bed are affected and the remainder can still provide pleasure and interest. The transplanting and temporary accommodation of plants does not become overwhelming. When further patches show the need for renewal, those already done will be maturing and contributing to the display. The necessary input of energy and expenditure is spaced out in 'easy instalments'.

Early spring is, in general, the time of lowest risk in transplanting and if there are many plants to be salvaged, then the restoration is best done at that time. Plants moved in autumn can succumb to early winter ills. They are wanting to rest, not to restore lost roots and heal wounds; they are thus more vulnerable to climate and prey to disease than those of springtime plantings, where the urge is to grow and develop, aided by improving weather. Whatever the time of year, when a refurbishment is completed it should be well watered and given close attention in further watering (and shading if necessary) until the plants have recovered.

It is not unusual for a planting scheme to go wrong, not because errors have been made in selecting the plants to be associated, but due to the unexpected behaviour of a few. Catalogues and reference books can only give a rough guide, in many cases, to the rate of growth and ultimate size of the plant and if a particular species finds the prepared conditions highly suitable, it may exceed

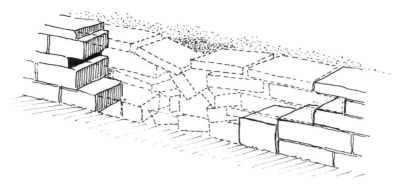

Figure 22 Wall repair—dismantling taken beyond damaged area

the text book size very quickly. Some growers can harden their resolve and dig out these over zealous specimens, however decorative or special they may be, but others are understandably reluctant to dispense with a healthy attractive plant. Measures can be taken to impose restraints without discouraging growth and flower too much. These are essentially pruning operations. Above the ground the more vigorous shoots can be cut back to about one-third of their length after the initial burst of spring growth and snipped again, if necessary, in the following months. Below soil level some root pruning is possible on those plants with substantial delving roots. Careful scraping round the crown of the plant will reveal many of the junctions where roots join the crown and up to half of these can be severed. It must be accepted, however, that these restraints have only a short-term effectiveness. Eventually the over-vigorous plant will either require removal in order to save those that it is threatening, or it will become so deformed and scarred from the repeated cutting-back operations that it is no longer worth retaining.

Occasional frost damage, collision with a heavy wheelbarrow or lawnmower, or a defect in the original building work, can all cause deformation or even collapse in a section of bed walling. Repair justifies more than just pushing the stones or blocks back into place and patching up with mortar. A quick repair of this type will never be satisfactory in either appearance or function; it will be weak against frost action and a blemish in the good looks of the bed. To make an effective repair the wall should be locally dismantled in the affected area and a little beyond (Figure 22). This may require some work with a hammer and sharp chisel to cut the mortar joints. Inevitably, the dismantling will create a small landslide in the bed filling and all the resultant loose material, plus any dislodged plants, must be collected and put to one side. All mortar adhering to the removed walling has to be cleaned off and this is most easily done using a wide-bladed chisel. If the stones or blocks are random in size and shape their original positions in the wall should be carefully recorded before removal, otherwise it is almost impossible to restore the walling to its former pattern. A rough sketch with a number given to each stone can be very helpful, the identifying number being chalked on as the individual stone is removed and stored.

The rebuild is little different from the original laying, except that where the replaced walling meets the untouched section there is a need for careful insertion and finishing of the mortar. After a day or so to allow for the setting of the joints, the wall will be strong enough to take the refillings of the repaired area with the soil mixture and any replanting needed.

Whilst not essential to the well-being of a raised bed, renewal of the top dressing from time to time does have its benefits. After two or three years mosses, liverworts, leaf debris and worm casts, begin to clog the open structure of the gravel or chippings used to surface the bed. Disturbing it with a small fork occasionally can delay the onset of the trouble, but it will happen eventually. It is not a great task to scrape off the 'infected' top dressing and replace it with new material. With the old dressing go all the unwanted invaders and clogging substances, plus weed seeds and soil pests, and the plants will appreciate the new clean surface with its excellent drainage.

In a much smaller way, occasional maintenance is needed to restore the top dressing where it subsides a little, particularly where it meets the inner edge of the walling. However well the filling was packed in and consolidated, this edge-slumping occurs to some degree. Happily it is only a matter of sprinkling a few handfuls where needed to restore the level, but if neglected it can progress to become a miniature crevasse between soil and wall, undermining plants and promoting erosion.

Plants for a raised bed

In preference to repeatedly describing the basic habit of growth for every individual plant in the following selection, I have presented them in sections, grouping those of similar character. I hope that this will also prove helpful to the reader, in choosing plants and deciding upon their placings and suitability as neighbours in planting schemes. Other information regarding flower colour, leaf form, lime tolerance, propagation etc. is provided briefly for each species listed. Also, in the interests of simplicity, those plants with persistent leaves, are identified as evergreens with suffix (E) to the name and the herbaceous types carry the suffix (H).

The time of flowering can only be an approximation, as it varies with prevailing weather as well as local climate, and it is therefore given as a period during which bloom might be expected to appear, in cultivation.

Many more could be added to this purely personal selection, but there are dozens of books devoted to the listing and describing of rock garden plants, available to those who wish for further knowledge, choice or inspiration.

Cushion-forming types — including others that make mounds of somewhat looser foliage

Acantholimon venustum   (E) June–July, 15cm (6in)
Loosely bunched, spiky leaves of silver-grey and flowering deep-rose. At its best in a hot, sunny place on the scree bed and appreciative of limy conditions.
Propagation. Difficult, but possible, from cuttings of young shoots, taken with a little old wood at the base. Easy from seed.

Armeria caespitosa   (E), May–June, 5cm (2in)
A dense mass of short, narrow leaves, which can be almost hidden in late spring by a covering of stemless pink flowers. Either scree or a light, stony soil mixture will be satisfactory, provided that the plant receives a generous amount of sunshine. The form *A.c.* 'Bevan's Variety' has deeper-hued flowers and a white-flowered clone is sometimes available. None of these objects to limy soil.
Propagation. Seed germinates readily. June–July cuttings of small shoots with some old wood at the base usually root well.

Campanula hercegovina   var. *nana* (H), June–July, 10cm (4in)
A small gem, with abundant starry flowers of wedgwood-blue over a thicket of wiry shoots bearing narrow leaves. Contented in any sunny scree and unusually long-lived for this genus. All too often it falls victim to slugs and snails just before flowering and should be protected accordingly.
Propagation. Rooted side-shoots can often be separated in July and grown on as young pot plants. Self-sown seedlings may appear quite some distance from the plant.

Dionysia aretioides   (E), April, 10cm (4in)
Although belonging to a genus of notorious difficulty in cultivation, this particular species can be grown in the open garden, given the midday shade of a rock and overhead protection in winter. A gritty, alpine soil mixture, or a fairly rich scree will meet its rooting needs. Grown thus it will slowly develop its bright-green, tightly packed mound of leaves and sport a scattering of golden-yellow flowers every spring. A limestone-dweller in the wild.
Propagation. Single rosettes, taken as cuttings in May, should root readily in moist sand. Seed is rarely set in outside culture.

Draba rigida   (E), April, 5cm (2in)
Tightly packed, bristly rosettes make up the smoothly contoured hump, from which rise numerous fine stems carrying small umbels of bright-yellow flowers. A good subject for a crevice, in full sun or partial shade. Unlike several other similar species, *D. rigida* will survive our winters without a covering. Limy soils are unsuitable but the plant will thrive in tufa.

57

Propagation. Unless other drabas grow in the vicinity, the seed that is set will usually germinate well and true, otherwise hybrids can be expected, but these are often well worth growing on.

Edraianthus pumilio   (H), June–July, 10cm (4in)
Grassy leaves of silver-grey crowd together under large, open bell-flowers of lavender blue, which are very like those of some campanulas. A general alpine soil mixture, or a not-too-lean scree (limy or acid) and plenty of sunshine, provide the right growing conditions. Not a long-lived plant in cultivation.
Propagation. Seed produced is usually true and germinates well. Cuttings of non-flowering shoots should be taken in June–July and rooted in moist sand.

Hutchinsia alpina   (E), May–June, 5cm (2in)
Freely produced umbels of clear white flowers, rise just above the contrasting dark-green foliage of densely packed, feathery rosettes. An easy plant to please, with usually, long life expectancy. Suitable for soil or scree mixtures with a low lime content.
Propagation. Easy from seed or cuttings of single rosettes.

Phlox caespitosa   (E), May–June, 5cm (2in)
A very neat and compact member of the genus, with flowers of a delicate pale blue produced in abundance and rising only a little above the foliage. The form *P.c. bryoides* grows even more tightly and is equally well-flowered. Well-drained acid soil and a sunny position are required, with no risk of dryness at the roots.
Propagation. Cuttings of young non-flowering shoots with lower leaves removed and taken in July–August.

Saxifraga cochlearis   (E), May–June, 30cm (12in)
Congested rosettes of lime-encrusted, grey leaves form a hard dome of foliage, which sends up graceful plumes of white, starry flowers on dark-red stems. A saxifrage for a limestone scree or crevice, where it can live to a great age, slowly increasing and totally hardy. Good resistance to drought and equally satisfied with sun or partial shade.
Propagation. Single rosette cuttings in July–August, or rooted fragments snipped from the edge of the plant.

Saxifraga ferdinandi coburgi   (E), April–May, 15cm (6in)
A fine example of the kabschia saxifrages with a tough constitution, suitable for the scree bed and enjoying limestone. The heads of golden-yellow flowers are carried on strong stems and hold their freshness and colour for two or three weeks.
Propagation. Single rosettes, taken in May as cuttings, should form young plants by October.

Thymus citriodorus 'Aureus' (E), June–August, 15cm (6in)

Golden leaves throughout the year give this plant great value as a permanent splash of bright colour. Any really well-drained soil in full sun will suffice. Very hard frost can cut it back to ground level, but it usually survives. Flowers are violet-pink, but not prominent.

Propagation. Rooted shoots, separated in June–July from the main plant and grown on as juvenile plants.

Plants forming a clump or tuft of more or less upright stems and foliage

Aquilegia bertolonii (H), May–June, 8cm (3in)

An easy and delightful dwarf columbine for the scree or general alpine bed. Rich blue flowers hang on short stems above deep-green leaves. Not long-lived, but rarely lost due to its habit of self-seeding, making propagation unnecessary.

Aquilegia flabellata (H), June–July, 15cm (6in)

Another small and dainty columbine, but in this case suited to cool, humus soils and partially shaded positions. The blue-green leaves are a perfect foil for the mauve flowers. The white-flowered form, *A.f.* 'Nana Alba' is often available from nurseries.

Propagation. Fresh seed sown in July–August usually germinates well. Old seed gives poor results.

Astilbe × *crispa* (H), August–September, 15cm (6in)

For semi-shaded, cool, moist positions in leafy soil mixtures. Dark-green, crinkled leaves and fluffy pink spikes of flower late in the season. *A.c.* 'Perkeo' is perhaps the most attractive of the varieties.

Propagation. Division of adult plants in April–May.

Clematis marmoraria (E), May–June, 10cm (4in)

A very uncharacteristic clematis from New Zealand, making a tuft of ferny foliage and flowering white on short stems. The seed heads are fluffy stars of a glossy pale gold. A crevice plant in nature and best treated as such in the general alpine or scree bed, with plenty of sunshine to promote good flowering. Indifferent to lime.

Propagation. Difficult, as seed is the usual means, but in cultivation the plant hybridises all too readily with other clematis.

Delphinium nudicaule (H), June–August, 25cm (10in)

Scarlet flowers are rare amongst rock plants, but this Californian species provides them in a long succession. Not difficult given a sunny placing in the general alpine bed with a low lime content.

Propagation. The generously produced seed usually germinates well, particularly if sown fresh, and is reliably true.

Dodecatheon pauciflorum   (H), May–June, 15cm (6in)
The cyclamen-like flowers of pale lilac, rise on upright stems from basal rosettes of semi-erect leaves. The plant behaves like a bulb, going dormant for the remainder of the year. A hot, sunny position in the general alpine bed is ideal. Other species, such as *D. jeffreyi* and *D. media* give alternatives for woodland conditions.
Propagation. Seed, or fragments of root pulled from the crown and grown on as rooted cuttings.

Erinus alpinus   (E), May–June, 8cm (3in)
A pink-flowered little 'rock-hopper' with a short, but merry life, self-seeding into nooks and crannies of the rockwork and easily culled if it becomes too exuberant. Anywhere in the rockwork or scree will meet its simple needs, limy or acid, sunny or lightly shaded.
Propagation. Very unlikely to be needed. Once acquired, *E. alpinus* manages its own continuation.

Gentiana septemfida   (H), August, 30cm (12in)
An upright species for the general bed, producing clusters of blue trumpets at a time of year when alpine flowers are less plentiful. It is prudent to choose specimens during flowering, as the blues vary in quality. The somewhat similar *G. lagodechiana* has single flowers and will often succeed where *G. septemfida* proves difficult.
Propagation. Best from seed, with a number grown on for colour selection.

Geranium farreri   (syn. *G. napuligerum*) (H), June–August, 15cm (6in)
Attractive green foliage with red edges to the young leaves and elegant flowers just tinted with pale lavender-pink. Prominent black stamens give the blooms a special beauty. Unlike many geraniums, this species is not over-vigorous for the moderately sized raised bed and is at home in either the general alpine or scree bed.
Propagation. Comes well and usually true from freshly collected seed.

Haberlea rhodopensis   (E), May–June, 20cm (8in)
A shady crevice, against a humus-rich, gritty soil, is the place for this slow-growing plant with broad rosettes of leaves and clusters of large lilac-hued flowers on radiating stalks.
Propagation. Seed is often successful, but the infant plants develop very slowly. Leaf cuttings give quicker results.

Hepatica triloba   (H), February–March, 15cm (6in)
A very early-flowering plant for light shade, tolerant of varying soil types and
by nature a lime-lover. Blue, pink and white forms are available. Crowded
single flowers rise just above the developing infant leaves, whose later sombre
green is often relieved by brown-purple mottling.
Propagation. Easiest using small divisions taken from the edge of an established clump, with minimum disturbance.

Lewisia rediviva   (H), June–July, 8cm (3in)
Although native to semi-desert terrain, this species does surprisingly well in
wetter environments. Acid scree-bed conditions are probably the best, with the
sunniest, hottest position possible. Foliage, looking like a green sea-anemone,
emerges in December–January and begins to die down as the huge solitary
flowers of clearest pink are opening to summer sun.
Propagation. From collected seed, as soon as it is ripe.

Linum   'Gemmell's Hybrid' (H), June–August, up to 25cm (10in)
Glorious golden flowers, produced successively through the summer weeks,
cluster on sturdy stems above grey-green leaves. For a sunny spot in the general
alpine bed. Unusually severe winters may prove fatal and overhead cover
makes no difference, hence yearly raising of cuttings is a wise precaution.
Propagation. April–May cuttings of soft shoots.

Papaver rhaeticum   (H), May–June, 10cm (4in)
A vivacious little poppy for the hot limestone scree, with a delicacy of form that
belies its toughness. It flowers successively for weeks, with silken-petalled,
golden blooms on slender stalks, seeding itself around very obligingly and
rarely to excess.
Propagation. Sow collected seed, whilst still fresh, in the spots where it will be
welcomed.

Penstemon scouleri   (E), June–August, 20–30cm (8–12in)
An open, bushy plant bearing large tubular flowers of handsome form with a
subtle, lilac tint. For an open position in the general alpine bed. Not long-lived
in cultivation, but easily sustained by prudent propagation. The white-
flowered form, *P.s.* 'Alba' has a cool, fresh grace of great value in any planting.
Propagation. Cuttings of half-ripe shoots taken in July.

Phlox   'Chattahoochee' (H), May–July, 30cm (12in)
A tangle of brittle, narrow-leaved stems, putting forth a long-lasting display of
large, powder-blue flowers, enhanced by an almost metallic sheen to the
petals. Happy in full sun or partial shade and with any reasonable well-drained
soil that is not too limy.
Propagation. Cuttings of half-ripened shoots taken in July–August.

Primula marginata   (E), April–May, 20cm (8in)

A plant to inhabit a stony cleft or acid scree, slowly extending its woody stems, clothed in attractively sculptured leaves with mealy coverings and carrying umbels of blue, primrose flowers. Varieties are abundant — selected for leaf patterning and range of flower colour.

Propagation. Young leaf rosettes plucked from the stems in June–July for rooting as cuttings.

Pulsatilla vernalis   (H), April, 15cm (6in)

The flower is a pearly goblet with a halo of fine, glistening hairs and the seed head that follows is hardly less beautiful with its whirl of fluffy fibres. No special attention or protection is required, other than to give the plant a sunny position in the general alpine bed.

Propagation. Seed loses its viability very quickly and should be sown as soon as it can be lightly pulled from the seed head (before it blows away!).

Ranunculus gramineus   (H), April–June, 20cm (8in)

Content in a semi-shaded or open spot and amenable to most soils, other than scree types. The foliage could be mistaken for a small clump of broad-bladed grass and its upright habit is a valuable contrast for plantings. Pale 'buttercups' are carried in loose heads on slender stems.

Propagation. Division of clumps in February–March.

Saxifraga fortunei   (H), October, 25cm (10in)

A delicate shade-lover for a humus-rich, acid soil mixture. Large rounded leaves strongly suffused with red-bronze, provide a dark foil to elegant spires of white, tasselled flowers in the late season.

Propagation. Division of clumps in April–May.

Soldanella montana   (E), March–April, 12cm (5in)

For a cool, fibrous, acid soil in dappled shade, with sound protection from slugs. Violet-blue fringed bells hang from strong stalks over round leathery leaves that hug the ground. The easiest of the Alpine 'Snowbells'.

Propagation. Rooted fragments taken from the fleshy surface roots, potted up to mature for subsequent planting.

Plants of prostrate habit, often forming dense mats of shoots and leaves

Anacyclus depressus   (E), May–June, 7cm (3in)

The feathery leaves are borne on radially spreading stems, which bear large white 'daisy' flowers at their extremities. A crimson underside on the florets gives the developing bud a rich colour, to contrast with the golden eye of those

blooms already open. The plant seems to be indifferent to the presence of lime in the soil, but needs plenty of sun for good flowering.
Propagation. Seed sown when fresh or cuttings from new growth in March–April.

Androsace sarmentosa   (E), May–June, 7cm (3in)
Equally suited in the general alpine bed or the not-too-limy scree and needing much of the day's sun to flower generously. A swarm of rich-rose flower umbels rises on upright stems from the congested mass of leaf rosettes. Self-propagating in 'strawberry' fashion, with short stolons rooting where their tips touch the soil.
Propagation. Snip off and lift young rooted rosettes in summer.

Antennaria dioica   (E), May–June, 5cm (2in)
A tight little carpeter, rooting as it spreads and giving freely of its fluffy pink flowers, which stand just above the grey-green foliage. A sunny patch of scree, limy or otherwise, will meet all the needs of this cheerful easy-going alpine.
Propagation. Extract rooted portions from the edge of the mat and replant where desired.

Arenaria montana   (E), May June, 15cm (6in)
The pure-white, starry flowers, enhanced by a lemon-yellow eye, are produced in abundance from a sprawling mass of narrow-leaved shoots. This species will adopt any scree or stony/sandy soil blessed with plenty of sunshine. An ideal subject for cascading over wall edges.
Propagation. Division and immediate transplanting in September. Cuttings from young growth in July.

Campanula raineri   (H), July–September, 8cm (3in)
Often regarded as an alpine-house plant, yet better pleased if given a place in a scree bed. Although coming from a limestone region, it does not demand lime in cultivation. Large china-blue bells sit on short stems above the grey-green leaves.
Propagation. Ease out underground runners and pot up short pieces for treatment as rooted cuttings.

Chiastophyllum oppositifolium   (E), July–August, 12cm (5in)
Previously known as *Cotyledon simplicifolia*, this is a useful plant for a contrast of form and a summer colour. The light-green leaves are fleshy and prominently toothed. 'Lambs'-tails', of tiny golden flowers are rich in clusters. Good for dry locations, but also quite content with any reasonably light soil in sun or partial shade.
Propagation. Cuttings of soft growth, taken in July or August.

Cyananthus lobatus   (H), August–October, 8cm (3in)

Valued for its late-flowering season, when deep violet-blue bells are produced from the tips of radiating stems. The leaves are small and rounded, crowding the fine shoots. Plants should be chosen when in flower to avoid dingy forms. For a lime-free leafy soil, in light or dappled shade.

Propagation. Cuttings taken in June–July should be over-wintered in a frame and planted out only when well established.

Dryas octopetala   var. *minor* (E), May–July, 5cm (2in)

The strong, creeping stems of rich mahogany colouring, bear little 'oak leaves' with a silvery-white reverse. Each flower is a creamy-white dish of overlapping petals with a striking cluster of golden stamens. Although a native of mountain limestones, in cultivation the plant will happily clothe any stony surface, given a very well-drained open soil (or scree) and a sunny spot.

Propagation. Self-rooted side-shoots can be detached and potted up for treatment as rooted cuttings.

Geum reptans   (E), June, 15cm (6in)

Not an easy plant to please but well worth trying in the general alpine or scree bed where, if responsive, it will send out its red stolons to increase the ground-hugging mat and put forth great golden flowers. Acid soils prevail in its habitats, and in cultivation limy soil mixtures should be avoided.

Propagation. By division, selecting robust, rooted fragments for growing in pots, July–August.

Hacquetia epipactis   (H), February–April, 12cm (5in)

A delightful and unusual plant for a shady bed. The clear-yellow, globular flower sits in a ruff of bright-green bracts and races the leaves to greet the spring warmth. With the blooms gone, the foliage still brightens a dull spot.

Propagation. Although it resents root disturbance, the plant can be increased by teasing away small divisions from its edges in very early spring, before growth is really underway.

Linaria alpina   (E), June–July, 5cm (2in)

Found at its finest, in form and colour, on the sunny screes of Europe's mountains. Not surprisingly it thrives on any open scree bed, covering its sprawling shoots with sprays of little 'snapdragons', each being a rich violet-purple with a bright orange lower lip. In cultivation the plant is more or less biennial, but usually self-seeding.

Propagation. May cuttings should root rapidly and form strong young plants for autumn.

Myosotis explanata   (E), July–August, 5cm (2in)

A white-flowered forget-me-not from New Zealand, which is very useful for any semi-shaded place on an acid scree. The blooms are stemless and spangle the tightly packed foliage with great charm.

1. A natural rock garden

2. The natural creation of tufa around a limestone spring

3. A trough devoted to a single species (*Androsace ciliata*)

Courtesy M. & H. Taylor

4. A 'built' trough incorporating an old stone seat

Courtesy RBG Edinburgh

5. Raised beds in the 'terraced' style

6. A young androsace flowering in its tufa cave

Mike Ireland

7. *Tsugotsuga taxifolia fletcheri* well established in a trough

8. *Tulipa batalinii* enjoying the drainage and warmth of a sunny raised bed

9. Two stones create a crevice for *Androsace alpina* in a raised bed

10. *Phlox nana* ssp. *ensifolia* in a well-matured hyper-tufa trough

11. Troughs in a group, combining attractiveness with ease of care

Courtesy D. F. Mowle

Courtesy W. Kirby

12. For a few years this copse of dwarf conifers will flourish as a trough feature

Mike Ireland

13. Young saxifrages incorporated during the building of the wall

14. Kabschia saxifrages are amongst the most suitable plants for tufa culture

Mike Ireland

15.   In a well-lit trough *Oxalis enneaphylla minutifolia* is long-lived and generous with blooms

16.   *Primula* 'Wanda' is an easy-going subject for a shaded raised bed

Alpine Garden Society Slide Library

17. The compactness and slow growth of *Douglasia laevigata* make it a good specimen for a trough or bed

Alpine Garden Society Slide Library

18. Campanulas revel in the sunny scree bed

Mike Ireland

19. *Saxifraga* 'Tumbling Waters' in a tufa bed

20. *Campanula zoysii* can be happier in a trough than in a pot

Propagation. Divisions of mature plants in April can either be directly planted out, or potted up for autumn transplanting.

Penstemon davidsonii   (E), June–July, 8cm (3in)

Rich, purple trumpets spring up from a dense flat mass of bronzed-green leafage, to create a swathe of colour wherever the plant has been introduced. In acid scree it will grow with moderate slowness, but given richer fare its enthusiasm can be excessive. A Californian — so by nature fond of sunshine.
Propagation. Take soft cuttings in July or August.

Potentilla nitida   (E), June–July, 5cm (2in)

Even when out of flower, the shining, grey-green foliage of this elegant carpeter warrants a place on the sunny limestone scree bed. Summer brings forth the clear-rose blooms to stand just above the flattering leafage. There are many poor clones in cultivation which flower sparsely, if at all, hence the plant should be sought when in bloom.
Propagation. Simply pull away tufts of already rooted shoots from the edge of the mat and replant where desired.

Primula hirsuta   (E), April–May, 8cm (3in)

Although the umbels of shell-pink flowers rise clear of the leaf rosettes, the whole character of the plant is compact and clinging. A lightly shaded crevice in the general alpine bed will meet the essential requirements, provided that the soil mixture is not limy.
Propagation. Division of clumps after flowering, or single juvenile rosettes used as cuttings in June–July.

Raoulia subserica   (E), June–July, 12mm ($\frac{1}{2}$in)

Minute silver-grey leaf rosettes form a living skin over the surface of a scree bed. In summer swarms of midget 'daisy' flowers stud the whole plant, later developing into fluffy seed heads. An acid or moderately limy scree mixture, with a clean top dressing, will ensure well-being and long life.
Propagation. Cut out rooted portions of the mat and replant immediately, March–April.

Bulbous plants — including those growing from corms, rhizomes and tubers

Allium oreophilum   July, 15cm (6in)

An easily accommodated bulb for the general bed or rich scree mixture, indifferent to lime, and asking only for a sunny location. A few grass-like leaves precede the slender flower stalks on which are borne flowering umbels of a delightful smokey-pink.

65

Propagation. Simple from seed, but requiring patience in the three years elapsing before the youngsters reach flowering age.

Cyclamen coum   January–April, 8cm (3in)
One of the two hardiest in the genus and suitable for a range of soil mixtures, accepting sun or light shade. There is a range of colour forms, from deep purple-rose to pale pink, with some interesting leaf variations.
Propagation. Self-sown seedlings are frequently to be had. Stored seed should be soaked in water for a day or so prior to sowing.

Erythronium dens-canis   March–April, 12cm (5in)
The nodding, reflexed flowers are reminiscent of small lilies and vary in colour from white, through several pinks, to a deep reddish-mauve, all with orange highlights at the base of the bloom. Mottling adds to the attractiveness of the simple pair of broad leaves. Easy in any well-drained, fibrous soil, with or without lime and tolerating light or dappled shade. Perhaps better pleased with full light in cooler gardens.
Propagation. Offsets from the tightly clustered corms are easily detached for growing on in July–August.

Fritillaria tubiformis   April, 12cm (5in)
A dwarf member of the family that sports a large nodding bell-flower of burgundy-red with prominent chequered patterning. Amenable to outdoor cultivation in a lightly shaded bed of cool, fibrous soil. The presence, or absence, of lime seems to be unimportant. *F.t. subsp. moggridgei* has a yellow flower.
Propagation. Not difficult from seed, but usually taking at least four years to achieve flowering size. Bulblets can be separated and grown on.

Hyacinthus amethystinus   March–April, 15cm (6in)
A delicate and refined bluebell, with none of the invasive habits possessed by those of our woodlands. The flower colour is not usually amethyst, but a clear, pale, sky-blue. Quite at home in the general alpine bed if the spot is sunny.
Propagation. Collected wild seed will give sure, but slow results. Alternatively, divide clumps in autumn and replant directly.

Iris histrioides   January–February, 10cm (4in)
The rich blue flower is decorated with a white blaze and a golden ridge on each of the falls. It rises in advance of the rush-like foliage, very early in the year and has remarkable resistance to bad weather. A slow-release feed, given at flowering time, should ensure the health and increase of a clump for many years, in a scree or general bed. Lime is appreciated, but not essential.

Propagation. Divide by lifting clumps in summer. Clean and store bulbs in dry, cool conditions. Plant out in autumn.

Merendera montana   September–October, 5cm (2in)
Closely related to the *Colchicum* and similar in the form of the flower, which opens at ground level before the leaves have emerged. Variable in colour from deep-rose to lilac-pink. The hotter the spot, the better it grows and blooms. A scree bed with low lime content provides a satisfactory home.
Propagation. Lift and divide clumps of corms in summer, or sow seed when fresh.

Narcissus bulbocodium   var. *citrinus* April, 12cm (5in)
Unlike many bulbs, the daffodils generally dislike a summer baking. This species requires a well-drained soil, in sun or dappled shade, with no risk of parching in the drier months. The nodding flower of primrose-yellow is long-lasting and cheerful in all weathers.
Propagation. Bulbs raised from seed should attain flowering maturity in three to four years. Natural increase below ground will provide bulblets for lifting and replanting in July.

Oxalis laciniata   May–June, 5cm (2in)
Equally satisfied in the scree bed or in a general alpine soil mixture, and needing full exposure to the sun. The spectacular flowers have an almost metallic glitter with dramatically pronounced veining of rich purple. They nestle, closely packed, in a delicate mat of finely divided, grey-green leaves.
Propagation. The curious, orange-pink rhizomes, lying at or just below the soil surface, can be very easily detached and replanted in autumn or early spring.

Trillium grandiflorum   April–May, 30cm (12in)
A plant of elegance and grace for an acid, humus-rich soil, in light or dappled shade. The white or faintly rose-tinged flowers are up to 10cm (4in) across and top the flower stem just clear of the foliage. The soft-green leaves, like the flower petals, are in threes, as the plant's name suggests.
Propagation. Trilliums are resentful of disturbance to their roots and as cuttings cannot be taken, seed remains as the prime means of increase.

Tulipa tarda   April–May, 8cm (3in)
A wonderfully responsive member of the tulip family, a single bulb producing several flowers, each of which is a white 'starfish' with a golden-yellow centre. Accepting any reasonable soil the plant will grow in full sun or light shade, slowly increasing both by underground division and self-sown seed.
Propagation. Sow fresh seed where the plant is wanted. Flowering stage is frequently reached in three years.

Dwarf trees and shrubs

This selection is offered with some trepidation as it includes *dwarf* conifers, many of which prove to be imposters once they have settled down in the garden bed. This matter is further complicated by the variation in growth rate from one garden to another and worst still, the fact that growth behaviour also depends upon which part of the stock plant has provided the propagating material. There can be a remarkable difference in the growth and behaviour of cuttings taken from the top, middle and base foliage of a single parent plant.

The shrubs listed are far less of a risk in cultivation, being naturally of small stature and not derived from aberrant growths, as are the conifers. Grafted plants can 'bolt' to unacceptable size, or be overtaken by the stock and disappear under coarser growth. It is consequently very important to the success of dwarf tree and shrub plantings that only specimens growing from their own roots should be acquired.

None of those selected is really suitable for the scree bed, but most will be adequately served by the general alpine bed or the cooler, humus-rich soils prepared for ericaceous and woodland types.

Suffixed to each species is the approximate rate of annual growth to be expected and abbreviated to ARG NO. cm (no. in), plus E or D to indicate evergreen or deciduous habit.

Berberis thunbergii   'Aurea', July, ARG 5cm (2in) D
Although this shrub *may* outgrow its setting after ten years or so, its golden foliage is of great value to the larger raised bed. The flowers are pale and lost in the brilliance of the leaves. In neutral-to-acid soils it will accept sun or light shade.
Propagation. July cuttings, but very difficult to root.

Chamaecyparis lawsoniana   'Gimbornii' ARG 2cm (1in), E
A little 'busby' conifer of dense leafage with a bluish cast to its colouring. Prefers acid soils.
Propagation. Make cuttings from shoots with a good proportion of new growth showing, in June or July. Use only material from the lowest part of the tree.

Chamaecyparis lawsoniana   'Minima Aurea' ARG 2cm (1in), E
Compact feathery foliage forms a broad spire of gold for all year colour. A well-behaved conifer.
Propagation. As for *C.1.* 'Gimbornii'.

Cytisus ardoinii   April–May, ARG 7cm (3in), E
A prostrate broom for a general or scree bed with acid soil and plenty of sunshine. Ideal for cladding wall tops or carpeting a flat rock. The flowers are a brilliant yellow and produced like a row of beads along each twig.
Propagation. Cuttings of half-ripe shoots taken in June.

Daphne cneorum var. ***pygmaea*** May–June, ARG 4cm (1½in), E
In complete contrast to the next daphne, this species forms a ground-hugging mat of fine-leaved stems. The intensely fragrant, pink flowers are held in clusters on the shoots.
Propagation. Take June–July cuttings of non-flowering shoots with the lower half of old wood.

Daphne retusa May–June, ARG 3cm (1¼in), E
Makes a squat bush with rhododendron-like leafage and is crowded with deliciously scented white flowers in late spring. The brilliant red berries that follow are very decorative, but poisonous. Best pleased by a neutral-to-acid soil, but will accept lime if the soil contains leaf-mould or peat.
Propagation. Extract fruit pips, soak for at least one day in water and sow immediately.

Euryops acraeus June–July, ARG 4cm (1½in), E
A stiffly upright, branched bush, clothed in silvered grey leaves and flowering with golden 'daisies'. With no apparent preference for limy or acid soils, it will grow equally well in the general bed or the scree, but must have a sunny position to give of its best.
Propagation. Detached suckers from around the base of the plant, or cuttings from non-flowering shoots in July.

Iberis sempervirens March–May, ARG 4cm (1½in), E
An easy-going sub-shrub of prostrate growth, giving generously of its white candytuft flowers for many weeks in the spring. Suitable for almost any type of bed if the location is not shaded. A very compact and slower growing form is *I.s.* 'Little Gem'.
Propagation. Cuttings of soft growth from June to August.

Lithodora diffusa June–August, ARG 8cm (3in), E
A sub-shrub with flowers of gentian blue and sprawling twiggy growth. Equally pleased in sun or partial shade, but demanding an acid soil. For those growers in limy regions there is another species, *L. oleifolia* which prefers calcareous soils and has blooms of less intense, but still lovely blue.
Propagation. Difficult, but not impossible, with cuttings taken from young shoots either in late July or early August.

Rhodothamnus chamaecystus April–May, ARG 2.5cm (1in), E
Few shrubs of dwarf stature can equal this mountain dweller, but it is not an easy plant to please and is extremely susceptible to root disturbance. The crisp, pink flowers are plentiful on the low, bushy growth and display their long stamens to great advantage. Limy or acid soils are suitable, provided that they remain cool and moist. In nature the shrub is rarely found in shady sites.

Propagation. From seed it is a long process requiring patience and hope. Cuttings taken with some mature wood at the base should be gathered in autumn and *may* root by the following spring.

Rhododendron
There are many dwarf rhododendrons perfectly suited to the rock garden, but the genus is vast and to pick out just one or two would be futile. Whole books and whole gardens are devoted to dwarf species alone, and it is to these that the reader should refer if the charm of rhododendrons is irresistible.

Further suggestions for raised bed plantings

Plants bearing the suffix (NL) have an aversion to limy soil mixtures.)

For the general alpine bed, containing a half-and-half soil mixture or something similar:

Aethionema schistosum	Pink, 10cm (4in), June
Allium cyaneum	Blue, 15cm (6in), July
Androsace carnea (NL)	Pink, 5cm (2in), April
Androsace sempervivoides	Pink, 8cm (3in), April
Anemone blanda	Blue, 8cm (3in), March
Aquilegia canadensis	Red, 15cm (6in), June
Artemisia rupestris	Yellow, 15cm (6in), June
Asperula nitida	Pink, 10cm (4in), July
Berberis buxifolia 'Nana' (NL)	Yellow, 40cm (15in), May
Campanula carpatica alba	White, 20cm (8in), July
Campanula cochlearifolia	Blue, 10cm (4in), July–August
Campanula 'Joe Elliott'	Blue, 10cm (4in), June–August
Crassula sediformis	White, 8cm (3in), June
Crocus chrysanthus	Yellow, 10cm (4in), March
Crocus fleischeri	White, 8cm (3in), March
Crocus medius	Purple, 10cm (4in), November
Cyclamen hederifolium	Pink, 10cm (4in), October
Cytisus procumbens (NL)	Yellow, 15cm (6in), June
Daphne arbuscula	Pink, 15cm (6in), May
Dianthus glacialis	Pink, 5cm (2in), June
Dianthus 'La Bourbrille Albus'	White, 2cm (1in), May
Dianthus 'Pikes Pink'	Pink, 8cm (3in), July
Diascia cordata	Pink, 20cm (8in), June–August

Erodium macradenum	White, 15cm (6in), June–September
Gentiana kochiana (NL)	Blue, 15cm (6in), June
Geum montanum	Yellow, 15cm (6in), May–June
Globularia cordifolia	Blue, 5cm (2in), June
Gypsophila repens	White, 15cm (6in), June
Helichrysum angustifolium	Yellow, 30cm (12in), August
Heuchera sanguinea	Red, 30cm (12in), June–August
Hypericum polyphyllum	Yellow, 15cm (6in), June–August
Incarvillea delavayi	Red, 25cm (10in), June
Iris reticulata	Blue, 25cm (10in), June
Lewisia cotyledon	Pink, 20cm (8in), June–July
Narcissus 'Tête-à-Tête'	Yellow, 20cm (8in), March
Oenothera glaber	Gold, 30cm (12in), July–August
Penstemon pinifolius	Scarlet, 20cm (8in), July
Penstemon roezlii	Rose, 15cm (6in), May–June
Primula elatior	Yellow, 10cm (4in), May
Primula halleri	Rose, 15cm (6in), May
Primula × *pubescens alba*	White, 15cm (6in), May
Saxifraga × *apiculata*	Yellow, 15cm (6in), March
Saxifraga 'South Side Seedling'	White/red, 30cm (12in), June
Saxifraga 'Tumbling Waters'	White, 60cm (24in), June
Scilla sibirica	Blue, 15cm (6in), March
Sedum spathulifolium	Yellow, 5cm (2in), July
Sempervivum arachnoideum	Pink, 8cm (3in), July
Tulipa batalinii	Cream, 20cm (8in), May
Tulipa linifolia	Scarlet, 15cm (6in), May
Zauchneria californica	Scarlet, 30cm (12in), September–October

For the scree bed:

Androsace albana	Pink, 10cm (4in), May
Androsace villosa var. *taurica*	White/pink, 4cm (1½in), April
Aquilegia scopulorum	Blue, 10cm (4in), July–September
Callianthemum kernerianum	White, 5cm (2in), March
Campanula allionii	Purple, 5cm (2in), August
Campanula arvatica alba	White, 5cm (2in), June–July

Campanula calaminthifolia	Pink, 2cm (1in), August
Campanula raineri	Blue, 8cm (3in), August–September
Cyananthus microphyllus	Blue, 2cm (1in), September–October
Dianthus callizonus	Pink, 10cm (4in), June–July
Dianthus neglectus	Pink/buff, 10cm (4in), June–July
Douglasia laevigata	Pink, 5cm (2in), June–July
Gentiana occidentalis	Blue, 8cm (3in), May
Geranium argenteum	Pink, 10cm (4in), July–August
Geum × *rhaeticum*	Gold, 8cm (3in), May–June
Globularia incanescens	Blue, 8cm (3in), June
Morisia hypogaea	Yellow, 2cm (1in), June
Oxalis 'Ione Hecker'	Pink, 5cm (2in), June–July
Petrocallis pyrenaica	Blue, 1cm (½in), May
Raoulia australis	Yellow, 2cm (1in), July
Saponaria ocymoides	Pink, 10cm (4in), May
Saxifraga cotyledon (NL)	White, 40cm (15in), June
Saxifraga × *elizabethae*	Yellow, 10cm (4in), March
Saxifraga 'Kathleen Pinsent'	Pink, 40cm (15in), June
Saxifraga oppositifolia	Purple, 8cm (3in), March
Sedum middendorffianum	Yellow, 15cm (6in), July
Sedum pilosum	Pink, 10cm (4in), June

For the cool, humus-rich bed:

Andromeda polifolia (NL)	Pink, 40cm (15in), May
Anemone nemorosa 'Allenii'	Blue, 15cm (6in), March
Aquilegia flabellata	Blue, 15cm (6in), May
Arctostaphylos uva-ursi	White, 15cm (6in), May
Calceolaria falklandica	Yellow, 10cm (4in), July
Calceolaria fothergillii	Orange, 10cm (4in), July
Cassiope lycopodioides	White, 5cm (2in), May
Colchicum autumnale	Pink, 12cm (5in), October
Cornus canadensis	Purple, 15cm (6in), June
Corydalis cashmeriana	Blue, 10cm (4in), May
Daphne blagayana	Cream, 20cm (8in), April
Epigaea asiatica (NL)	Pink, 10cm (4in), May

Fritillaria pallidiflora	Yellow, 25cm (10in), May
Gaultheria trichophylla	Pink, 8cm (3in), May
Haberlea rhodopensis	White, 8cm (3in), May
Kalmiopsis leachiana (NL)	Pink, 20cm (8in), April
Leucojum autumnale	White, 15cm (6in), September
Narcissus cyclamineus	Yellow, 10cm (4in), March
Phyllodoce nipponica (NL)	White, 15cm (6in), April
Primula edgeworthii	Mauve, 8cm (3in), February–March
Primula reidii var. *williamsii*	Blue, 12cm (5in), May
Primula rosea	Rose, 15cm (6in), April–May
Primula vialii	Mauve, 10cm (4in), May
Ramonda myconi	Blue, 10cm (4in), May
Saxifraga umbrosa 'Clarence Elliott'	Pink, 8cm (3in), May
Soldanella carpatica	Blue, 8cm (3in), March–April

3 Troughs

The stone trough, hewn from a boulder or a quarried block is an ancient artefact and for many centuries was the only form of strong and durable container. It took various forms, predominantly worked and finished just enough for the purpose and no more, but occasionally, like the church font, refined for ceremonial use. The Saxons made coffins cut from a single slab of rock, which are still being unearthed and show little deterioration since the days of their completion.

Even when heavy earthenware troughs and sinks became widely available the stone version was still being produced, favoured by farmers for its greater weight and immense strength when used for the feeding and watering of livestock. Early in the present century apprentice stonemasons were still tested by being given a rough block from which they were expected to produce a finished pig trough in a single day's work.

Although the majority of 'genuine' troughs are of sandstone and particularly millstone grit, they have been fashioned from many types of rock. In the Cotswolds and Yorkshire Dales they can be found in all shapes and sizes, hacked out from solid limestone and in the Welsh hills there are troughs built from slabs of slate bound with iron and sealed with lead. Huge granite troughs, found in Scotland, are relics of the old leather tanning industry and throughout Britain other wonderfully worn and scarred specimens bear witness to their use as quenching baths in the work of the blacksmith.

A century ago there must have been many thousands of stone troughs still in use in farms, dairies, breweries, stables and a host of other places. Where have they all gone? Even though 'genuine' troughs are now very fashionable and sought-after in contemporary gardening, this cannot fully account for their massed disappearance. They are still discovered here and there, usually by accident or by those who are unusually alert and perceptive. Three large and oddly shaped stone steps intrigued one gardener so much that he finally levered one over, and the other two very quickly afterwards. Each was a perfect trough, inverted for the new use some 50 years before. Old walls occasionally contain similar hidden treasure.

In hill-farming areas, where stone is usually plentiful, derelict troughs can still be found, sometimes almost buried at the base of a spring or by a barn wall, hidden under weeds and rusty scrap. Although these finds may look abandoned they belong to somebody, and detective work is often needed to locate that person. If this is successful don't expect the rightful owner to be ignorant of the

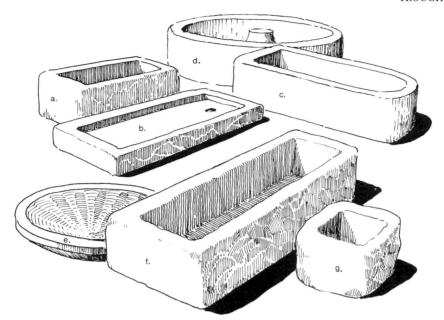

*Figure 23 A selection of troughs and similar artefacts **a**. pig trough, **b**. sink, **c**. pump trough, **d**. millstone, **e**. quern stone, **f**. water trough, **g**. post stone*

trough's market value, and be sure that it can be got from where it is to where you want it, before making a reasonable offer.

Most forms of troughs are suitable for planting or can be made so. Their shapes and depths are varied, suiting them to different types of plant. The most common forms are the pig trough, which is broadly rectangular and a full hand deep; the pump trough, usually with one end rounded and up to twice the depth of the pig trough; the water trough, which can be almost any shape and size; and the very shallow slab-shaped sink. Less often seen are the 'Chinaman's Hat' querns, dished millstones and post stones, none of which are troughs, to be precise, but serve equally well when given a drainage hole or two.

Even broken or badly cracked troughs can be made good with the help of modern adhesives. There are preparations on the market specially formulated for the bonding of stone and concrete. Provided that the break is not complex and there are no pieces missing, a trough can be restored to use just like a broken tea-cup by glueing it together. The word 'genuine' has been used here to define troughs and trough-like articles, crafted in years gone by for specific purposes and now utilised as garden features. They are, in a sense, antiques put to good use. There are, however, other forms of trough, fabricated from various materials in various ways, some imitating the real thing, others achieving a satisfying effect through clever use of stone.

Such is the present popularity of the trough that both professionals and amateurs are now producing the 'authentic' article masoned from solid stone, but taking advantage of modern cutting equipment. First of all, of course, a suitable block of stone has to be acquired. Old farm gateposts, of the monolithic type, have been successfully transformed into troughs, as have other massive masonry blocks. The use of powered cutting tools compensates for an important difference between the old craftsman's task and the present one. Masons made their troughs from freshly quarried stone, in what they called the 'green' state. This virgin material is softer and easier to cut than it is after a period of exposure to the air, when chemical changes take place and permanently alter the properties of the stone. Limestone in particular undergoes this marked change within six weeks, which is why an old block will blunt the best of chisels after only a few blows and responds erractically to the desired direction of the cut.

Powerful abrasive wheel cutters make light of such problems. They can be seen slicing through concrete kerbstones in a matter of minutes or 'sawing' their way through a brick wall. Masonry drills can be had in a range of diameters and lengths and will do sterling work before needing sharpening. Both of these tools are used to great effect in making troughs. Figure 24 shows how the wheel cutter can be used to slice down into the stone to create the basic edges of the trough interior. Following this initial cutting there are variations in the method for removing the rectangular core created.

The wheel can be further used to produce cross-cuts, requiring great care and control to avoid overcutting. Steel wedges are then hammered into the cross-cuts to split out rough chunks for removal. Alternatively, a large masonry drill can be used to produce a 'chain' of holes into which a stout, wide-bladed chisel is then driven to do the splitting. With either method the base of the resultant hole is extremely jagged and uneven and it is then a matter of patient work with hand tools to even out and smooth the cavity. A selection of chisels will ease this work and one of them should be the multi-pointed type illustrated in Figure 24, being indispensable for the major part of the work, including the final smoothing. Professionals can resort to power chisels to greatly speed up the work, but their use is really getting beyond the capabilities of most amateurs. In the hollowing out of small troughs, wheel cutters can be too big for the work but the masonry drill method is ideal.

Wheel cutters create an astonishing amount of dust, which is extremely fine and smothers everything in the vicinity, including the user. Goggles and a dust mask are absolutely essential and heavy gloves are needed to protect the hands from flying stone particles. Anyone using this type of cutter for the first time should definitely seek tuition and then try some practice cuts before touching that precious block of stone.

A far gentler and hazard-free method of producing a trough is to 'build' one. It gives a free rein to creative ideas for shape, size and appearance and can be done in a leisurely fashion, using easily handled materials and the minimum of tools. Basically it is a miniature wall built around the edge of a slab, which can be a paving stone, or one cast in concrete to a desired shape. There is no need to drill drainage holes in the slab as these can be incorporated at the base of the wall, just as they were described for the raised beds. Figure 25 shows a typical

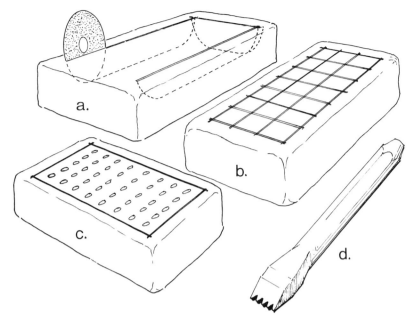

*Figure 24 Stone trough manufacture **a**. abrasive wheel cutter used for sides and ends **b**. cross-cutting to form splitting segments **c**. hole drilling to form splitting segments **d**. multi-point chisel*

construction where fragments of thin stone have been mortared together on a flat stone base. The walling material can be got from a variety of sources. Sea-shore or river pebbles produce interesting effects, as do broken slates and even pieces of roof tile.

A development of the same idea, on a larger scale, leads to some fascinating innovations. The problem of finding a slab big enough for a base is overcome by

Figure 25 A 'built' trough made from a slab and mortared fragments of stone (drainage outlets in lowest course)

building from ground level around a suitable container. A domestic water tank or even an old bath can serve this purpose. Both come with a drain outlet in the bottom, which solves one problem immediately. Baths have legs and so the base is raised above ground level, but water tanks and the like need to be stood on bricks to give drain water a free exit. Having set up the tank or bath and poured in a bucket of water to check that none fails to drain away, it is simply a matter of walling around it. The variations on this theme are many when considering how many containers could be so employed. A sawn-off plastic dustbin would produce a circular trough and baby baths are often a pleasing oval or pear shape. It is not necessary to pack the space between wall and container with mortar; dry sand or gravel is easily poured into the gap and will do the job of stabilising the structure and keeping out mice, snails and other would-be occupiers. This type, of course, is immovable and built on site.

Troughs built from slabs are functionally no less effective than other types, but they are not regarded as decorative or attractive by most gardeners. This is probably due to the starkness of the slabs, however handsome the stone or slate may be, and the inevitable fastenings needed to hold things together. The moulding of troughs has almost become an art form, or perhaps more accurately, a modern-day craft, which is now regarded as a part of rock gardening. It holds a fascination for many and has inspired some ingenious developments and innovations.

A substance christened hypertufa is the basic material employed and this was literally invented by an eminent member of the Alpine Garden Society. Its original use was as a substitute for the naturally occurring tufa, which has always been in limited supply and expensive. Sand, cement and sieved peat were mixed together and water added to produce a consistency resembling stiff porridge. This was then roughly moulded into rock-like forms and allowed to set. It was surprisingly successful and whilst it never achieved the appearance of true tufa, it did look very much like weathered stone after a year or two, and what is more, plants could be grown *in* it as well as around it.

It was not long before its full potential was realised and hypertufa troughs began to appear. The early models were cast in simple moulds contrived from cardboard boxes used very cleverly. Figure 26 illustrates how two selected boxes can be used to form a rectangular mould, the inner one forming what will be the cavity of the trough and the outer forming the exterior. The sizes of the boxes should be such as to give a wall thickness of about 5cm (2in) in the mould. A similar thickness is needed in the base. The hypertufa mixture is made rather wetter than previously described so that it will just about flow when it is tipped into the mould. The base is put in and levelled first, then the inner box is placed on it, central to the outer box, and filled with dry soil, sand etc. to prevent it from caving in later.

More mixture is then pushed down the gap between the boxes to form the walls of the trough and tamped down with a blunt stick to rid the mixture of any air pockets. Unless the outer box is of very stout cardboard it will need some support, for as it becomes wet the weight of the mixture will cause it to belly outwards and, at worst, split at the seams. A few bricks placed against the sides before filling will prevent such disasters, but some deformation will occur, which is all to the good in the final appearance.

Wet fabric is then draped on the whole thing to ensure a slow setting and curing of the mixture for maximum strength. After about 36 hours the mixture should have cured sufficiently for the finishing work to be done, and here the trough maker can apply creative vandalism. The wet covers are removed and the now soggy outer box peeled away to expose the side faces, showing some sharp corners, imprints of cardboard etc., which must be removed. The hypertufa at this stage should carve like chalk and so, with old knives and a stiff brush, the hard edges are removed and the surfaces textured. How far to take this artificial ageing and softening is at the discretion of the maker; it need only be a rounding and blending of the corners and a vigorous brushing of the sides, or chunks can be sliced away to give a really rustic effect after a final brushing. The interior needs less work as it will be hidden but the all-important drainage holes must be cut and this requires removal of the inner box. When most of the soil or sand filling has been scooped out, the remains of the box can be extracted to give access to the base of the trough. The drainage hole, or holes, are cut using an old knife, twisting it like a screwdriver to bore through the base. With these tasks completed the trough is again covered with its wet shroud and left for a further two or three days, after which it will be strong enough to be moved and a week later it can be filled and planted.

There is no precise recipe for the hypertufa mixture. It has been varied to suit different ideas and uses, but the most commonly preferred proportions are, by volume, 1 part cement, 2 parts coarse sand, 1–2 parts moss peat passed through a quarter-inch (6mm) sieve). If the peat content is increased significantly it will

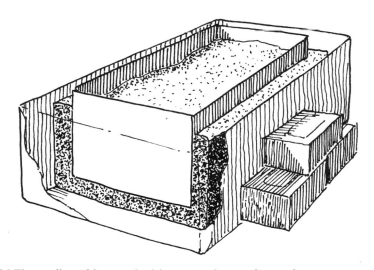

Figure 26 The cardboard box method for casting hypertufa troughs

weaken the hypertufa too much for trough making. An increase in cement will produce a harder, stronger substance looking much like weathered limestone. More sand will reduce strength, but improve appearance. In all cases the sand should be as dry as possible before mixing commences.

If there is an unused patch of ground available, a trough can be cast in a pit. The method requires only one cardboard box to form the interior, the exterior being moulded by the excavation. Wonderful gnarled and aged effects can be imparted to the outer faces of the trough by the roughness and texture of the sides of the pit. As in the two box method the gap between pit and box should not be much less than 5cm (2in) to give sufficient strength to the finished trough. For the casting the mixture is first laid in the bottom of the pit and to gauge the thickness, two or three twigs are pushed into the base earth and cut to 5cm (2in) high to act as depth indicators. They will be entombed in the trough base, but to no ill effect. Upon the base is placed the box, filled as before with sand etc. and the sides of the trough can then be filled and tamped. All that remains is to put a cover over the site and to leave everything undisturbed for three days. At the end of this period the trough can be exhumed by carefully digging out the surrounding earth sufficiently to allow handling. A fence post or suchlike is then used as a lever to ease one end of the trough upwards and a chock put in place. On no account should the sides of the trough be subjected to levering or other forces at this stage, as they are relatively weak and easily fractured.

The now tilted trough in its enlarged hole should be accessible for inspection and any necessary touching up. Earth can be brushed off the sides to reveal the character achieved and the hypertufa should still be soft enough to allow any unsightly knobs or blemishes to be knocked and scratched away.

To complete the curing process and hence achieve full strength, the trough should be left as it is for four or five days, then it can be fully removed from its hole with the aid of levers and a bit of manhandling. After a clean up it is immediately ready for planting. Obviously there is a sensible limit to the size of trough suited to this method, imposed mainly by the work of getting the finished article out of the ground. Anything much bigger than 60 × 45 × 30cm (24 × 18 × 12in) can (from sobering experience) cause problems.

So far hypertufa has been employed in bulk form but it can be used as a surfacing material to make some unlikely objects look like stone. The best known of these is the disguised glazed sink. Thousands of these have been discarded in the modernising of kitchens. Dimensionally they are ideal troughs and they are ready fitted with a drainage hole in the right place, but the shiny white porcelain is quite unacceptable in the garden. Hypertufa, applied as a coating to all the visible surfaces, can bring about a transformation. After a year or two of weathering the coating accumulates stains and tiny growths and at a few paces distant is indistinguishable from mellowed stone.

For coating, the cement, sand and peat mixture is made rather stiff by reducing the added water a little, so that it has the feel and behaviour of wet plaster, but like that substance, it will not stick to the glazed porcelain. Early enthusiasts patiently chipped off the glazing to expose the granular surface beneath and this held the coating well, but now modern adhesives have provided an easy alternative to that laborious method. The type of adhesive is frequently labelled 'Universal' and marked as a PVA compound. Before it is applied the whole sink must be thoroughly washed and rinsed to clean off all grease and dirt. When dry the surfaces to be coated should be painted with the special adhesive, allowing some overlap onto the base and interior. After a little time the adhesive becomes tacky to the touch and it is then ready to receive the coating, which is patted on in handfuls to an approximate thickness of 12mm ($\frac{1}{2}$in). It can be modelled during this laying on operation to resemble stone that has been weathered, or worn by years of usage.

The coating should be taken a little way under the base and down the insides to protect its edges from attack by the weather and consequent separation of the hypertufa from the glazed surface. Like the cast trough the coated sink should be covered with damp fabric, protected from rain and left for four or five days before being put into use.

By the porch of a cottage in Cheshire stands a charming small trough packed with a thriving collection of compact, slow-growing alpines. It takes close inspection to confirm that it is not a product from the nearby and long-abandoned quarry, but hypertufa. Its shape and size give no clue as to what lies beneath the stone-like exterior — a polystyrene fish box! Improvisation and hypertufa have been used to create many novel and successful troughs and new ideas come to light every year.

The life of the coating varies considerably, depending on the quality of the original work and the weather. Frost is the main enemy, working its way between the hypertufa and the surface that it is coating, eventually causing cracks and flaking. It is possible to render repairs to damage of this kind and involves cutting away the damaged coating back to where the bond is still sound. Adhesive and fresh mixture are then used, just as in the original work, to restore the affected area. By comparison the cast trough is everlasting, there being plenty of examples aged from 20 to 30 years, which have suffered nothing except a progressive improvement in their appearance.

The job of slapping-on and texturing hypertufa holds much of the fun recalled from childhood adventures with mud and clay, but it needs a note of caution. Some of the chemicals present in the mixture play havoc with bare hands and thin rubber gloves are a wise precaution.

A more massive form of the coated trough can be built in a manner similar to that employed for the earlier described table bed. It is not a movable unit and so must be made in the place where it is to stand. Small piers are built on simple foundations to support one or two slabs. These can be large pavings or stone flags, symmetrical or informal in shape. A wall is then raised around the edges using any suitable material such as bricks, concrete fragments or even builders' rubble. The appearance is unimportant, as the coating will fully conceal the wall and in fact roughness in the build can both aid the coating work and the final looks of the trough. In order to maximise the strength and durability of the whole structure, it is best to apply the coating to the inside surfaces of the wall as well as the outers, taking it down to meet the base. When the coating has been completed, it should be left for two days to cure under damp coverings and then textured with scrapers and brushes to the desired extent. A further curing of three days will render the coating sufficiently strong for the filling and planting to go ahead. There is no need for bonding adhesives in this application as the roughly built wall will provide an adequate key for the applied hypertufa. The coating thickness will vary on the uneven wall surface.

The scale and proportions, shapes and texturings of coated troughs are open to imaginative design and the utilisation of many materials, One of their great assets is that they can be purpose-built to suit a particular location or planting.

Another innovation, which does not fit into any of the types described, is literally hand-made round a shaped core of chicken-wire. The latter is folded and squeezed to form the basic size and shape wanted and a generous quantity is used so that there are three or four layers mangled together in the sides and base. Chicken-wire is easily worked with fingers and thumbs, hence a fairly tidy 'bird's nest' of crumpled wire can be produced, free from protruding ends and edges (Figure 27). Hypertufa mixture of a stiff consistency is then pressed into the core so that it thoroughly penetrates the tangled wire. Further handfuls are applied until the core is no longer visible and the surfaces can be modelled and textured just like a coated trough. The finished article should then be stood on a flat base, over which a plastic sheet or newspaper has been spread, and left to set and cure in the usual way.

If the shaping and texturing has been well done in the final stage of forming the trough there is no need for further work at the semi-cured stage, save for perhaps a light brushing over to remove loose particles and smooth out any

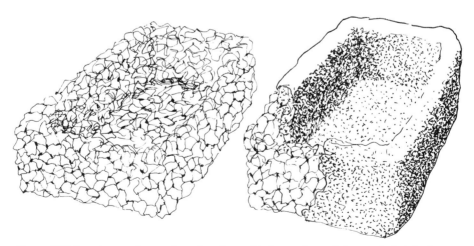

Figure 27 The wire-mesh core for a hand-moulded trough, and the partly finished article

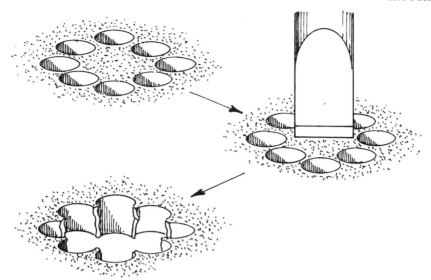

Figure 28 Chain-drilling to form a drainage hole

finger marks etc. This method produces a very strong trough with the durability and long life of the cast type, the chicken-wire acting to some degree like the steel bars within reinforced concrete.

Some of the trough types described lack the all-important drainage holes, and here again modern tools make light of what used to be a task for the skilled mason. In a small trough a single hole is sufficient and it matters little whether it is in the centre of the base or at one end. The size of the hole in a small trough need be no more than 12mm (½in) in diameter and can be bored using a masonry bit if a heavy-duty electric drill is available. Failing this the hole can be made using an ordinary DIY drill and a smaller bit, by producing a ring of holes (Figure 28) and knocking out the centre with a blow from a chisel; the roughness of the hole produced is unimportant. Large troughs are better served by two drainage holes spaced well apart and 2.5cm (1in) or so in diameter.

Moving troughs

Troughs cast in boxes or pits and those built on small to moderately sized slabs, usually have to be transported to their place in the garden and for all but the very lightweight ones, this requires some aids to muscle power. It is worth remembering, whilst devising the method for moving, that although the hypertufa appears hard and rugged, it is nevertheless brittle and easily fractured by careless handling. If there is a good paved surface running between the place of manufacture and the intended site of the trough, a stout sack truck will move all but the larger troughs easily and safely (Figure 29a). If

83

possible, the truck used should have soft-tyred wheels to further ease the operation. Soft ground, such as a lawn or a gravel-covered path, impedes wheeled transport considerably, often to the point where progress is impossible and it is necessary to lay down a temporary track. This need not span the whole route, but can be laid in relay fashion as the load moves forward. Pieces of plywood, old doors or planks will suffice and only need cover a few strides.

Where the weight or size of the trough exceeds the capabilities of a truck, ancient methods come to the rescue. Again, unless the route is hard and evenly surfaced, a temporary track is needed and in this case strong planks are essential. The trough is moved along on rollers (preferably of strong steel tubing) and although these can bear directly onto its base (Figure 29b) it is far safer and more efficient to put together a simple cradle from scrap timber (Figure 29c). A good, sound lever is the prime mover in the system and its first use is to jockey the trough onto the cradle, a job that requires care, patience and fingers kept well away from any gaps. For this stage it is better not to have the rollers already in place beneath the cradle, otherwise the latter is very likely to move off when the trough touches it. Once loaded the cradle can be levered up to receive the rollers and then propelled forward by pushing, if the going is easy, or by repeated thrusts of the lever at the rear end. As 'used' rollers emerge from behind the progressing cradle they are collected and placed ahead on the track. Similar reuse is made of the track sections as they come clear. If this task is done by only one person a reliable chock is a vital piece of

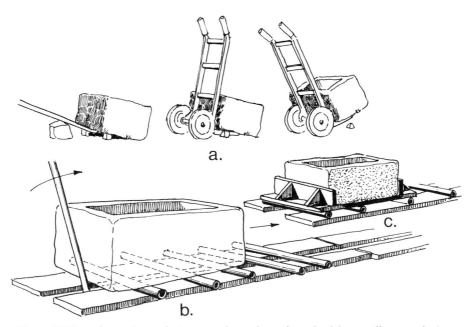

a.

c.

b.

Figure 29 Trough-moving techniques **a**. *the sack truck method for smaller troughs* **b**. *the plank-track and roller system for larger troughs* **c**. *the 'cradle' improvement for system 'b'*

equipment, needed to prevent the cradle and its burden from quietly rolling back or forward whilst unattended. Even though the track may look level this danger is always present and a derailment or collision after a few seconds of runaway travel can ruin the work of days. All the methods described apply equally to stone troughs.

With the final arrival at the trough's resting place comes the problem of getting it onto its support, which may be ready prepared or built as part of the setting up operation. Techniques employed will be dealt with later when discussing the various types of support.

Siting the trough

Much of the advice already offered for the positioning of raised beds can be applied equally well to troughs. The plants grown in them have essentially the same likes and dislikes, requiring the avoidance of overhanging foliage, harsh winds, excessive heat etc. There are one or two points of difference, mainly due to the smallness of the trough in comparison with a bed and its insularity. The volume of soil mixture contained in a trough is much less than that held in a raised bed, and it is not in contact with the ground. These two differences cause a more rapid drying-out in the trough, which can influence its placing. Areas in full sun and open to drying winds can cause a small trough to become parched in a single day under certain conditions. If the gardener is regularly on hand to make good the moisture loss by timely watering, there is no real problem, but many are unable to give such attention. Unavoidable daily absence or frequent periods away from home can be reasons for placing the trough where the light is good but there is shade during the hottest part of the day. For similar reasons it may be prudent to plant sheltering shrubs nearby to give protection from drying winds. Troughs can look well against a house wall, but such sites should be checked first. South-facing walls can produce a broiling environment in their immediate vicinity and dry strips along walls are common due to the sheltering effect of broad eaves on the roof above. Wind can be deflected into violent eddies by walls and fences, and troughs placed by them, in the belief that they would be sheltered, may actually suffer more than those in more open situations.

If the siting is by a path or drive, it can be a grave mistake to have the trough protruding. Bumps from vehicles or wheelbarrows are often very damaging and the trough is well placed to retaliate by bruising knees or ankles. Any position close to the route used by refuse collectors, paper-boys and delivery men is at high risk from unintentional bashing and scraping.

It may be that only a single trough is required, to perhaps form the centrepiece of a garden design, hence the question of where to put it does not arise, but the attraction of trough gardening is strong and the featured specimen is unlikely to remain solitary. By one means or another more troughs are acquired and they become a collection, requiring thought as to how they can be placed to the best advantage.

There are basically two ways in which a number of troughs can be set up in the garden, the first being to dot them around to create points of added interest in the general scene. The second is to display them as a group in a prepared setting. Where they are sited individually there can be some contriving of the surroundings to complement the trough's character or the plants it contains. A brown sandstone or well-weathered hypertufa trough is emphasised by a close background of silver foliage and a built trough is softened by allowing dwarf mat-forming plants to creep around the base and a little way up the sides. A group of troughs looks at its best when occupying a space with a minimum of distractions. Roomy paved areas, if made from quietly toned material, offer an excellent setting of this type, nowhere better seen than in the Royal Botanic Gardens of Edinburgh. Here each trough is set in a little island in the paving and planted round with low-growing alpines. This approach lends itself well to a generously sized patio, provided that the troughs do not have to compete with pots of pelargoniums and begonias, or an intrusive barbecue hearth! Areas of lawn put to the same use are invariably unsuccessful, the troughs forming an obstacle course to any type of mowing equipment and constantly in danger of a head-on collision with it. Sometimes a 'waggon train' of troughs can be seen flanking a driveway or edging a terrace, an arrangement which somehow robs the troughs of their charm and gives them the look of a children's ride.

In general, troughs are planted with sun-loving species accustomed to mountain soils, but they can also be devoted to plants requiring cooler root-runs and some shade. Their sitings have to take account of these needs and are quite different from the open aspects discussed so far. Dense shade is too much for the types of plants suited to trough culture, for it pleases only those species with leaves specially developed for low light levels. These are predominantly large and out of scale with the small area of the trough.

Dappled shade such as that cast by adjacent deciduous trees, permits sufficient light to satisfy a range of plants, including both woodland dwellers and some mountain species that favour the shadier sides of outcrops and cliffs. An alternative to dappled shade, which will also be acceptable to the plants mentioned, is partial shade. This refers to an area that receives sun only in the cooler hours of the day, either in the morning or late afternoon and evening. The shadows of buildings and dense trees can produce the desired effect. If leafage is used as the source of shade it can be near the trough but must not form a canopy over it, otherwise drips, moulds and pests will rain down upon the luckless occupants.

Supporting the trough

Few troughs are seen sitting on or close to ground level, the common preference seeming to be for some sort of plinth or pedestal. There is no good argument to justify this practice, other than that the ornamental or architectural appearance is improved, for it is of no benefit to the plants. Nevertheless, the majority of trough owners prefer the elevated support and there are certainly situations where it can be an enhancement. Practicalities impose some limits to the height of a support, the major one being that the trough has to be lifted on to it. To keep within the practical means and equipment available to the great majority of us, the support must allow the trough to be manoeuvred into position without the need for a hoist or mobile crane. Alternatively, the support may be built progressively as the trough is raised little by little, with the help of simple levers and chocks. Another limitation on height is the stability of the whole structure, which is inherently top-heavy.

The supports, which are pleasingly in proportion to the trough carried, are usually of a height less than that of the trough itself and often just about half of it. They can be built in advance of, or during, the final placement, and this option can be influenced by the size and weight of the trough. The materials used for the support are important; a handsome trough can be disfigured by a hotch potch of brick-ends and shards of tiles beneath it. Nothing excels matching stone for a stone trough, and it is worth some trouble to obtain what is, after all, a small quantity of the right material. Failing this, good quality synthetic stone will suffice and time will improve its looks. Plain, grey concrete is always at odds with whatever it supports, but it does not blend too badly with hypertufa or built troughs.

A single attractive block used as a support requires virtually no preparation other than some levelling and firming if it is to sit directly on the earth. By contrast a built pedestal involves some work. If seated on earth and carrying a heavy trough, it may be necessary to put in a rudimentary foundation, but generally this is seldom needed. The use of mortar in built supports is uncommon and usually only found in tall supports where it adds to the stability, or where the available stone is unevenly shaped and impossible to firm up by other means. In most cases a squat rectangular column is built 'dry' from regularly shaped or masoned stones, packed where required with thin flakes of stone or slate to correct any wobbles and to achieve a reasonably level and even top. Often this construction leaves a hollow core, which is filled with gravel or sand to add stability without hindering drainage (Figure 30a).

As yet only single supports have been considered, but twin types are equally popular and require less material and skill to erect (Figure 30b). Long troughs can look better on these double plinths, whereas those that are square or almost so, sit uneasily, giving the appearance of having fat, stubby legs. At the other extreme small paving slabs are set up on edge to form slim piers, but these fail to match the solidity of the trough.

Assuming that the trough has been safely ferried to its permanent site by truck or rollers, it has to be married with its support. If the latter is already built and the weight of the trough allows it, a quick lift by one or two fit people completes the operation, but working single-handed or with a weighty trough can call for some engineering. For the ready-prepared support a slow, but sure method is to raise the trough alongside and when its base is level with the support top, to work it carefully across. The raising is done levering up first one end and then the other, pushing packing pieces (chocks) beneath each time.

Repetition of these operations brings the trough up to transfer height. It is then a matter of swivelling one end of the trough until it is partially resting on the support, then moving the other end and so on until the transfer is complete. This is not an easy task and it frequently dislodges some of the support, but rectification is relatively easy when the trough is safely in place. The option is to raise the trough in the same way by alternating leverage at each end and inserting pieces of the final support instead of temporary packings. (Figure 30c). By this method, the support is built as the trough rises and the transfer operation is eliminated.

None of that which has just been described is either easy or without risk of minor injury, and it can be almost wholly avoided if the trough is set up nominally at ground level. On a paved area this can entail nothing more than sitting it on two thin strips of slate or even durable wood, just to allow the drainage water to escape. Alternatively, a slab or two of the paving can be removed and the depression filled with stone chippings. The trough can then be sat directly onto these. Drainage water can get away unhindered through the stones, which can be left as they are or planted with easy-going creeping plants like thymes, sedums and sempervivums. On sites other than paving the two strips beneath the trough are rather more substantial, but as they will be partially buried in the earth and hidden, any uniformly shaped stone or brick will suffice. Again, plants can be grown around the trough to form a flattering carpet of foliage and flower.

To all that has been said on the matter of supports, two important points must be added. Before filling and planting a trough it should be checked for

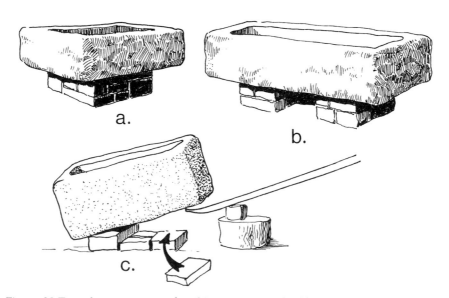

Figure 30 Trough supports a. pedestal b. twin piers c. building the support on site

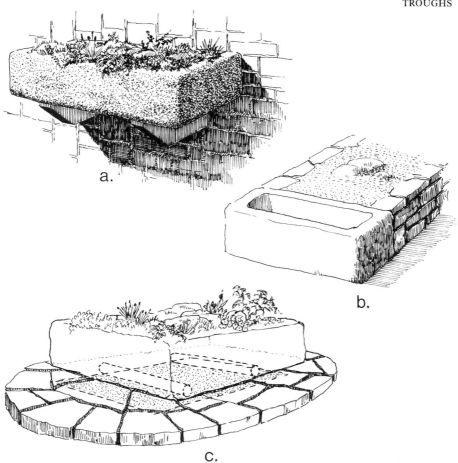

*Figure 31 Less convential supports and placings **a**. wall-mounted trough **b**. bed-end
mounting **c**. a movable support for a 'disguising' trough location*

stability and any movement corrected by the insertion of packing pieces under
the base. At the same time, the complete run-out of water should also be
confirmed and this may require additional packing, or a modification to
reposition or remove any supporting pieces obstructing the drainage hole.
Away from the more conventional supports, special arrangements are met with
where a trough has been wanted in a particular place where plinths and piers
are unsuitable. Figure 31a shows an unusual mounting devised to hold a small
trough on a wall, the two stone bearers being built-in and hence very secure.
The same figure also shows a trough incorporated in a raised bed to form an end
and a sink used to camouflage an inspection cover. In the latter example two
rollers have been left in place to allow easy movement of the sink and the stones
forming the surround are close-fitting but unmortared.

Filling the trough

For the purpose of filling, a trough (unless huge) can be likened to a large flowerpot, offering a strictly confined root-run to the plants contained, and disposing of surplus water through a hole in its base. Also, like the plant pot, its contents will warm up more quickly, dry more quickly and freeze more quickly than the soil in a garden bed. Soil mixtures prepared for troughs have to take some account of these matters and in consequence are different from those used in raised beds. The sparse mixture recommended for scree beds, for instance, would dry out much too rapidly in a trough and the food supplies would be exhausted in a very short time. Fortunately, the trough possesses some unique properties which are not fully understood, but work to the benefit of the plants. It is possible to use 'richer' soil mixtures that would be less than ideal in other situations, thus improving the moisture retention and food reserves of the trough's filling. The immaculate drainage and the limited space within the trough may contribute to processes that allow this enrichment, but whatever the true reasons might be, it is an accepted characteristic of stone and hypertufa troughs. Glazed sinks and troughs with impervious linings, such as plastic, behave similarly, but to a lesser extent. They require a little more drainage material in their filling mixtures, possibly due to condensation effects on the inner walls.

For scree and crevice plants a reliable mixture in trough culture is equal parts (by bulk) of sterilised loam, leaf-mould or peat, coarse sand and 4mm chippings. In Britain an equally effective alternative is a half and half blend of John Innes No. 1 or No. 2 potting mixture and 4mm chippings. For the first mentioned mixture a little plant food should be added in the form of slow-release fertiliser (low in nitrogen), applied at the manufacturer's recommended rate for seed composts. Alpines from rather more fertile habitats will prosper in an even richer blend with the chippings content reduced to half of that specified above. Troughs filled entirely with leaf-mould have produced remarkable results with plants requiring humus-rich soils, such as Asiatic primulas. Where the planting is devoted to bulbous species, mixtures used for potting produce equally good results in troughs.

Prior to the introduction of any mixture for the filling operation, a little preparation of the trough's interior needs to be done to ensure that the drainage will be fully effective. For many years it was believed that a substantial layer of crocks or stone chippings covering the base was essential, but trials have shown such to be excessive. It is only necessary to protect the drainage hole from blockage and to achieve this it is first covered by a few shards from a broken plant pot or a piece of perforated zinc of the meat-safe type. Over this, or the shards, a handful of gravel is heaped, forming a crude coarse filter to hold back the filling material, but not the escaping water. Taking care not to disturb this outlet protection, the filling material can then be introduced.

Just like the raised bed, a trough will suffer settlement of the filling after a period of time and the same countermeasures apply. When filled, planted and top dressed the trough should look over filled, its finished surface being humped and at all points higher than the edges of the trough. The apparent excess slightly marring the looks of the final arrangement, will decline surprisingly quickly, and by the end of the first year its value will be clear. Whilst some light firming of the mixture during filling is all to the good, it is useless to pound and compact it in the belief that this will prevent any future settlement. This is not so and furthermore the drainage will be impaired. For safe and adequate firming, press down with a loosely clenched fist on the soil surface.

Surfacing

The small area within the trough is not suited to surfacing with large stone fragments and if too many, or oversized dwarf rocks are used to produce an effect, there can be insufficient space left to accommodate the plants. In an average sized trough or sink, two or three stones no bigger than a fist are ample to produce a miniature outcrop and perhaps create a crevice or two. Badly chosen chippings can mar the whole appearance and scale of the planting. The type of stone used does not seem to matter so far as the plants are concerned. Even so-called lime-haters are unperturbed by a top dressing of limestone, probably because there is so little of it and hence its effect is negligible. More important is the depth of the top dressing if it is to function properly in providing a perfectly drained surface layer, slowing down water loss from evaporation and discouraging weeds. To these ends a minimum of 18mm ($\frac{3}{4}$in) is necessary, even though the trough may be shallow. The surfacing is best applied after all planting is complete, otherwise much of it will either spill over the sides, or disappear into the soil mixture during the digging of planting holes.

The choice of material for top dressing is less influenced by what is locally available. So little is required to surface a trough that the gardener can afford to be very selective. Some types of turkey grits are ideally sized for both soil mixtures and top dressings, and have the benefit of being clean and free from dust. One material which never looks quite right is pea gravel, the very rounded small pebbles often seen on sale as bottom covering for aquaria. These can give a funereal look to the trough, especially before the plants have spread and mingled.

Proportions

The trough holds a pocket of soil within strict and impenetrable boundaries, as far as the roots of plants are concerned, hence its proportions are a major consideration in planting. At the extremes, the depth can be a mere 5cm (2in) in the shallow stone sinks, or a luxurious 60cm (24in) or so in some of the giant troughs.

The shallow sink is perhaps the most difficult to furnish with a satisfactory selection of plants. Only a very limited number of species will tolerate the thin,

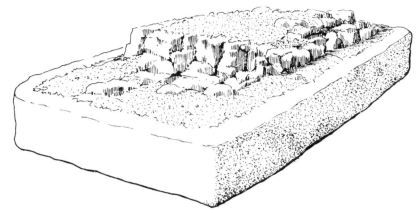

Figure 32 A plateau formed in a shallow sink

quickly parched wafer of soil that is offered. Some steps can be taken to improve matters a little, the most common of which is to build up a plateau using a few stones (Figure 32), thus increasing the soil depth over a portion of the area. The same principle is employed, but in an all-over manner, where a dwarf wall is built on the edges of the sink; however, the final effect is not to everyone's liking. Tufa is a useful material for improving the growing capacity and this method will be described later. Heaping the soil mixture and support-ing it with small rocks, produces an unattractive and improbable-looking miniature landscape, which is prone to collapse and rapid erosion under the effects of heavy rain.

Deeper troughs allow a far greater scope in planting and where the soil depth exceeds 15cm (6in) most of the dwarfer mountain plants will be satisfied with the available root-run.

Although species needing humus-rich soil mixtures are unlikely to accept troughs offering little depth, very few of them root down more than a few centimetres, and so provided that their moisture needs are met consistently, they will be content with 10–15cm (4–6in). In fact, depths beyond this may be less satisfactory, as a layer of 'unused' soil mixture lying beneath that exploited by the roots can become sour and actually harmful to the plants.

Protection

Troughs are often used to cultivate plants of particular value, for reasons of rarity, habit or unsuitability for the open garden. The isolation offered by the trough allows for more individual attention and protection, including the often required winter cover. The provision of a cover is relatively straightforward. It can be of glass or transparent plastic and should be sized slightly larger than the trough top. The securement against wind is critical and warrants careful attention, as the cover is light in weight and easily lifted. Figure 33 illustrates three types of cover and the measures taken to hold them down. All are equally effective in both protecting the plants and staying put in boisterous weather.

The first is simply a pane of glass propped over the trough, with suitably sized stones used as supports and secured by a strong wire encircling both trough and cover. The wire should be made as taut as possible when fitted and then

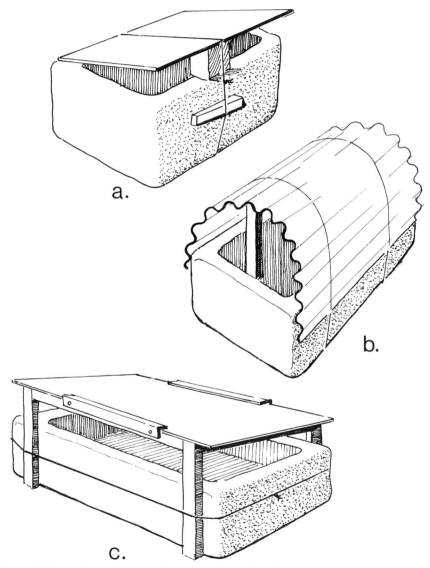

*Figure 33 Trough covers **a**. simple glass and chock with tensioned hold-down wire **b**. plastic tunnel with end props and hold-down wires **c**. wooden support frame for glass or plastic cover*

tensioned further by pushing in one or two wedges between it and the trough side. Cord or thin rope, whatever the material might be, is less satisfactory than wire due to its elasticity and response to differing weather conditions. However tight it may be when fitted there is always subsequent loosening and hence shifting of the cover. If only thin wire is to hand it should be wrapped around several times to achieve adequate strength.

The second type utilises a corrugated plastic sheet, curved to form an arched roof over the trough. To prevent it from slipping down the sides of the trough and a consequent loosening of the securing wires, two small wooden props are pushed in at each end, as shown. The securing wires again pass completely around the cover and the trough, then are tensioned as before.

The four-legged support shown as the third type, can be used for either glass or plastic covers. it is simply fashioned from 2.5cm (1in) square section timber to fit a particular trough. Where glass is the covering material a few wooden holding strips are added to secure the glass pane to the frame top. Plastics can be battened and nailed. The legs are sized to touch the ground and hold the roof just clear of the highest point of the trough's contents, with a slight slope to shed water. A wrapping of tensioned wire, holding the legs firmly against the trough walls, completes the work.

None of these types has any permanent components which must be left in place and so can be dismantled after each winter and stored for reuse, year after year.

Maintenance

One of the many attractions of trough culture is the very small requirement for maintenance. With the trough firmly seated in place and its occupants established, there is little else to do other than enjoy the results. The only call for prompt action is when damage occurs, by accident, weathering, flawed construction etc.

Very occasionally a stone or cast hypertufa trough can suffer a fracture sufficient to cause major breakage, such as the loss of a corner or even an end. The use of modern specialised adhesives has already been mentioned as the means of repair in such cases, but the same substances are just as effective for less dramatic damage. Flakes of stone knocked from a trough by a carelessly swung spade or a badly steered lawnmower can be replaced if they have not shattered. Cracks can be filled and their progress checked by the use of weatherproof bonding and filling preparations.

The deterioration of hypertufa coatings is usually in the form of flaking away from whatever they are covering and is most prevalent on corners, edges and where the coating terminates. If the damage is widespread then a complete stripping and recoating will be far more satisfactory than a rash of patchings, but localised blemishes on an otherwise sound coating are worth repairing. The procedure starts with a careful chipping away of the afflicted area, working outwards to a little beyond the limit of damage. The next step is a repeat of the original coating method on a small scale. using, if possible, the same sand and peat of the original mixture, a small quantity is prepared whilst the bonding agent is drying to the required tacky state. The latter is applied not just to the bared surface of the underlying sink, box or whatever has been used, but also to the edges of the surrounding coating. All that remains then, is to pat the patching mixture into place and protect the repair from the weather for a few days whilst the setting and curing takes place. If the weather is dry a light spraying with water over the patched area, once or twice a day, will ensure that the curing takes place at the correct rate to produce a strong and durable repair. The same technique can be employed for minor damage on cast hypertufa troughs.

Once a year the integrity of the drainage should be checked. Silting-up of the filtering material covering the drainage hole can occasionally occur, causing the trough to become soggy with excessive retained moisture. The fault is not readily apparent and plants can suffer harm before it is eventually suspected. A simple test is to water the trough thoroughly and then inspect the flow out of the drainage hole. If this is sluggish or insignificant a restrained poke up the hole with a large nail will sometimes clear the blockage, evidenced by a sudden outflow of the retained water. Failure of this quick remedy calls for nothing less than an emptying of the trough and a refurbishment of the drainage.

However well the top dressing was originally prepared and applied, it will eventually lose its essential properties due to the action of worms and infiltration by growths of moss, liverworts and other tiny weeds. Rather than waiting for such depreciation to become obvious it is preferable to renew the top dressing on a routine basis. In Britain's moist climate it is safe to say that renewal will become necessary after about two years.

Eventually, after several years, a 'tiredness' will become apparent in any trough community, which no amount of plant food will cure and it is then that the trough should be emptied, refilled with new mixture and restocked.

Plant Replacement

Other than the attentions described there is little else needed in the way of maintenance, save for the watch on weeds and pests, but occasionally drastic action may be called for when a particular plant proves to be far more vigorous than expected and threatens the whole community. Pruning back the offender wins merely a temporary victory and the only fully effective remedy is removal. In the confines of a trough any attempt to root out the entire plant is bound to cause widespread disturbance and it is far less hazardous to sever the principal roots just below the surface and remove everything above that level. A small hole can then be cleared to take what is hoped will be a better behaved replacement. The same approach can be applied where established plants have failed, but if the casualty is only young it is usually sufficient to carefully dig it out with a small trowel. In all cases the replacement planting should include a little fresh soil mixture fortified with a pinch of fertiliser, to compensate for the nutrients taken up by the replaced plant.

Trough plantings rarely mature to plan and often leave small unoccupied spaces in an otherwise satisfactory group. As an alternative to attempting the squeezing-in of nursery plants as fillers, a few young seedlings or even a pinch of seed can be put in with negligible disturbance and later thinned out to leave the strongest individual to grow on.

Planting a trough

Whereas rock-garden beds are usually furnished progressively as suitable plants are acquired, troughs are generally planted completely in a single operation with a carefully selected community. There are sound practical reasons for doing so, for if plants are inserted in ones and twos over a period of some months the early arrivals tend to claim all the rooting space. With this advantage they are well entrenched and developing new growth by the time that additional plants are introduced and the latecomers face strong competition. By contrast a single full planting gives equal opportunity to each individual and also eliminates the disturbance and damage that is inevitably caused by periodic additions.

It can be a mistake to completely fill a trough with soil mixture before introducing the plants; the digging of holes, spreading of roots and final firming all becomes increasingly difficult as the work of planting progresses. The roots of plants already installed may be disarranged or wounded and it is hard to avoid unevenness in the finished surface. If 10 per cent of the filling mixture is temporarily put aside such risks and frustrations can be greatly reduced. With the level of the soil mixture a little below the trough's rim it is easier to arrange the plants and their root systems. A hole will take the lower part of the roots and when loosely filled in gives some stability to the plant, but still allows adjustments to position and depth. When all of the new occupants have been

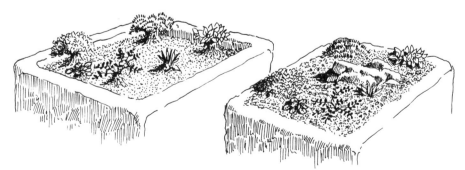

Figure 34 Trough planting, showing the incomplete filling and partially buried root systems, followed by final topping-off and surfacing

Figure 35 A trough for crevice plantings, featuring vertical flakes of stone packed with soil mixture

semi-planted in this way the reserved soil mixture can be spread around them, worked into their upper roots and levelled off. At this stage there should be a little root still exposed as an allowance for top dressing (Figure 34). The latter is applied first to each plant, and carefully worked under it with the fingers until it is firmly supported, after which the remaining surface can be covered and smoothed over. If miniature rocks are included in the planting arrangement they can be set in position and made stable before the top dressing is put on.

There is a modification to the planting preparation that caters specially for small crevice plants, both in meeting their needs and displaying them very attractively. When the trough is no more than half-filled with soil mixture, thin plates of stone are set on edge quite close together, to produce a humped outcrop. Further soil mixture is packed around and between the stones, whilst at the same time, young plants are inserted and made firm. Figure 35 shows a trough planted in this manner.

Labelling

A surprising number of otherwise well-planted troughs are marred by a flock of prominent labels giving them the look of miniature cemeteries. There are two practical ways of avoiding these disfigurements, one being to draw a simple plan of the trough and on it write the names of the occupants. Alternatively, if the name is written in pencil, the label can be pushed down into the soil until only the tip remains visible. Burial seems to have little effect on the writing, even after two or three years and at any time the label can be partially

97

withdrawn to reveal its information. A further benefit is that rearrangements by inquisitive birds no longer occur.

Feeding

The 'when, what and how much?' of feeding trough plants is little different from that of raised-bed culture. The types and rates of application for fertilisers are the same, although a little more care is often needed to prevent spillage onto the plants. Because the amounts involved are small and the work is light and easy, liquid feeding is often used even though it is required more frequently. This illustrates how the trough is treated more like a potted plant than a small garden bed.

Watering

The flowerpot analogy is again relevant. Troughs can become quite warm during summer days and consequently lose moisture more rapidly than the cooler ground they stand on. This loss is amplified when the trough is made from porous stone or hypertufa, where the evaporation is from all the exposed surfaces, just as happens in a clay pot.

The burrowing of a finger beneath the top dressing will quickly ascertain the moistness, or lack of it, in the underlying soil mixture and anything less than just moist to the touch signals the need for watering. If the troughs are arranged as a group then it is feasible to use a sprinkler and hose to treat them en masse, but if they are displayed as single specimens, here and there, the watering-can is the only practical implement to use. If it is possible to see water escaping from the drainage hole this is an excellent guide to watering, for when the drain is flowing the trough should be thoroughly soaked. Where the drain outlet is hidden, then for safe measure give each trough (unless small) something approaching a gallon ($4\frac{1}{2}$ litres) of water, for it is hardly possible to over-water, but so easy to give too little.

In Britain, troughs with winter covers are very unlikely to need watering during the time they are so protected. There is usually sufficient inward seepage to maintain an adequate moisture content in the root-run. A monthly probe with the educated finger will reveal the state of the trough's filling and if water is required it should be given only moderately and without wetting the plants too much.

Holiday absence spells danger to troughs, especially as it usually occurs in the summer months, when just a few days of sunshine can dry out those that are shallow or small. Again the grouped collection wins out in being suitable for sprinkler coverage and the automatic on-off system. Lacking help from neighbours, the owner of the scattered trough collection has help at hand in the self-regulating drip-feed systems, which can be arranged to serve each trough individually to maintain it in a moist condition. These will continue to work whatever the prevailing weather, but are very unlikely to cause any harm and will certainly allay concern about drought.

Plants for troughs

To avoid complications, it is assumed that the soil mixture used to fill the trough will be neutral in character, i.e. with a pH of around 6.5 to accommodate the widest range of plants. Only where a particular species *needs* a higher or lower pH will mention be made.

All the plants listed will tolerate frequent rainfall whilst they are active, but during dormancy a few require overhead protection and this is noted where it applies.

Some duplication will occur between the following selection and that for tufa, where certain plants are equally suited to both forms of culture.

Androsace alpina   (E), April–May, 2cm (1in)
A low cushion of crowded leaf rosettes, which is well covered with sessile pale rose flowers, when given a sunny position in a very well-drained soil mixture. The plant dislikes limy soil. Protect in winter.
Propagation. Sow seed in December and leave exposed to the weather. Take small branchlets as cuttings in May.

Androsace cylindrica   (E), March–April, 5cm (2in)
More robust than *A. alpina*, making a domed cushion of dark-green leaves and producing a froth of pure white flowers on short stems. Protect in winter.
Propagation. Easy from seed sown December–January, or from single rosette cuttings taken in May.

Androsace lactea   (E), April–May, 10cm (4in)
A taller, looser growing species flowering in open umbels of the clearest white. Easy to please regarding soil and aspect and more vigorous than the denser types.
Propagation. Usually produces self-sown seedlings, otherwise collect seed and sow immediately.

Androsace pyrenaica   (E), March–April, 5cm (2in)
One of the tightest and slowest growing members of the family, making a congested hump of tiny rosettes which can be almost hidden by a swarm of close-growing white flowers. A little shade from the hottest sun will prevent scorching of the cushion in summer. Limy soils are resented. Winter cover is a wise precaution.
Propagation. Cuttings of single rosettes are viable, but difficult due to their smallness. Seed usually germinates well.

Campanula zoysii   (H), May–June, 2cm (1in)
A very choice and intriguing bell-flower with tubular flowers of slightly violet-blue, hanging in tidy bunches over the wandering mat of small glossy leaves. Happiest in limy soil mixtures and like most of the genus, fond of the sun.

Propagation. Take short lengths of the sub-surface runners and plant them up as rooted cuttings in a very gritty soil mixture.

Chamaecyparis obtusa 'Nana Minima' (E)
A truly dwarf or even midget conifer that is very unlikely to outgrow any medium-to-large trough in the gardener's lifetime. Makes a tiny 'plum pudding' of tightly packed foliage.
Propagation. June–July cuttings taken from the tree's base, with half their length being young, actively growing wood.

Chamaecyparis obtusa 'Pygmaea' (E)
In 30 years this low, flat conifer may achieve a height of 60cm (24in) and a spread of 90cm (36in). The foliage is browny-green and makes feathery whorls.
Propagation. As for 'Nana Minima'.

Daphne petraea (E), May, 20cm (8in)
The single exception to the avoidance of grafted dwarf trees and shrubs, for whilst this beautiful species will grow on its own roots, it does so at a frustratingly slow rate.
  Crowded branches and twigs bear tufts of narrow leaves, each of which can produce the gloriously scented, rose pink flowers to smother the whole tiny bush. At no time must there be a lack of moisture at the root, nor must the place be shaded if the bloom is to meet expectations. Best suited to the larger troughs.
Propagation. Small, non-flowering branches grafted onto sturdy seedlings of *Daphne mezereum* (or other species) in January.

Dianthus microlepis (E), May–June, 5cm (2in)
A tight little 'hedgehog' of grey-green leaves, with small pink flowers freely dotted over its surface. Limy soil and sunshine produce the best results.
Propagation. Cuttings of single shoots from July to August.

Dionysia aretioides (E), April–May, 8cm (3in)
The only species of a difficult genus that can be grown and flowered outdoors with some confidence. Needs the shady side of a stone, where it will slowly increase its soft cushion and put out its plentiful primrose flowers. Protect in winter.
Propagation. Single rosettes taken as cuttings in late May.

Douglasia montana (E), June, 5cm (2in)
Forms a neat green cushion of fine leaves which is covered in early summer with a mass of closely held, deep-rose flowers. For a sunny trough with a generous depth of root-run.
Propagation. From self-produced seed, or cuttings of half-ripened shoots taken in July–August.

Draba dedeana   (E), April–May, 10cm (4in)
Papery-white flowers make a snowy cap over the sombre-green cushion of this Spanish crevice plant. It is a martyr to aphids and should be checked frequently. Easy to please given a sunny perch.
Propagation. Seed is reliable and cuttings made from single rosettes should root well.

Draba polytricha   (E), April–May, 15cm (6in)
The moss-like cushion is a fresh green and sends out numerous heads of bright-yellow flowers on slender stems. Although it may survive winter wet in our drier regions, a November-to-March covering is good insurance.
Propagation. Cuttings can be taken in June, using small clusters of rosettes, but seed normally produces young plants just as quickly.

Edraianthus pumilio   (H), May–June, 5cm (2in)
A sun-loving, tufted plant with grassy leaves of pale grey. The flowers are large, upturned lavender bells, which sit in clusters amongst the foliage.
Propagation. Cuttings can be made from young tufts of leaves separated from the plant in July. Occasionally self-sown seedlings appear around the plant.

Edraianthus serpyllifolius   (semi-E), May–June, 5cm (2in)
The creeping habit of this species can be used to good effect in crevices and overlapping the trough edges. Bell-flowers of a rich violet are massed on the dark-leaved prostrate stems.
Propagation. Cuttings of side-shoots in July–August.

Gentiana angulosa   (E), April–May, 8cm (3in)
Often appearing in catalogues as *G. verna angulosa*, it is more amenable to cultivation than *G. verna* and just as brilliant in the blue of its trumpet flowers. Parching spells serious damage and even death.
Propagation. Division of clumps can be carried out in July–August, but the safest means is to gather and sow seed immediately when it is just ripe.

Gentiana saxosa   (E) July–August, 5cm (2in)
White, goblet-shaped flowers stand upright on a mat of dark-green leafage giving the whole plant a very attractive, cool beauty. Apart from a dislike of lime, it has few fads and is an easy, charming subject for any sunny trough.
Propagation. Sow the generously set seed as soon as it is ripe.

Gentiana × stevenagensis   (H), September–October, 15cm (6in)
An 'Autumn Gentian' for the larger trough with a humus-rich, acid soil filling. The purple-blue flowers are massed over a finely leaved carpet of foliage.

101

Dappled shade produces the best results in general and a summer feeding will ensure good blooms.
Propagation. Ridiculously simple, requiring only a lifting, and replanting of clumps in April.

Hedera helix 'Marginata' (E)

A miniature, contorted ivy, which in addition to being an excellent subject for rockwork, can be planted in the soil adjacent to a ground-based trough, to cling to the outside with a wonderful softening effect.
Propagation. Take cuttings of ripe stems in July.

Helichrysum sessiloides (E), April, 5cm (2in)

A grey-leaved hummock with a profusion of white 'everlasting' flowers sitting tightly on the foliage. It benefits from winter protection in wetter regions, but is otherwise perfectly hardy. For health and good flowering the planting spot should be sunny, hot and low in lime content.
Propagation. Taking cuttings of leaf tufts in June or July.

Hypericum anagalloides (E), June–July, 5cm (2in)

The plant forms a prostrate mat of small, round grey-green leaves upon which sit almost stemless flowers of an orange-yellow. Too much sun can cause distress, so a place in partial or light shade is called for.
Propagation. Soft cuttings, taken in June or July.

Iris winogradowii (bulb), February–March, 8cm (3in)

Unlike many dwarf iris this species prefers a semi-shaded location, where it will open its golden-yellow flowers just clear of the soil surface, well ahead of the sparse, upright leaves.
Propagation. From seed or division of bulbs in July.

Jasminum parkeri (E), June, 25cm (10in)

A dwarf shrub for the larger trough, slowly developing a congested mass of twigs which is spangled with clear-yellow flowers. Later in the year these produce little black berries. The hardiness is questionable in cold, wet districts.
Propagation. Use young shoots for cuttings in July–August.

Juniperus communis 'Compressa' (E), annual rate of growth 12mm ($\frac{1}{2}$in)

A well-known and much-used 'Noah's Ark' or 'Candle Flame' juniper, which although something of a cliché in trough culture, is nevertheless ideal, growing slowly and with the reliable symmetry to form the familiar 'Cypress' shape.

Propagation. Base cuttings of growing shoots with mature wood at the lower end. Can take a year to root.

Narcissus asturiensis   (bulb), February, 10cm (4in)
Variable in form and height, but always delightful and totally hardy, this tiny daffodil is easy-going as to soil and situation and is best left undisturbed to slowly increase below ground.
Propagation. Lift and divide bulb clusters in June and replant immediately.

Oxalis adenophylla   (H), May–June, 8cm (3in)
Just above the delicate foliage a host of satiny-pink flowers open to every sunny period and roll into tubes of resting petals at other times. To obtain the maximum pleasure from this plant it is essential to give it a sunny position.
Propagation. Divide the bulb-like rhizomes in autumn and replant immediately.

Phlox nana subsp. *ensifolia*   (H), June–July, 20cm (8in)
A straggly stemmed, spectacular plant for a roomy trough in full sun. The huge flowers are a pastel pink and centre on a conspicuous white eye. Limy soil is resented.
Propagation. Gently unearth and cut away lengths of root-bearing growing shoots. Pot these up for treatment as rooted cuttings (May).

Phyteuma orbiculare   (H), June–July, 10cm (4in)
The strange flower of this crevice plant looks like a cluster of minute, blue wine bottles and lifts only a little above the saw-edged leaves. A lime-lover in nature, but accepting neutral soils in cultivation.
Propagation. Autumn division is possible, but unreliable. The sowing of fresh seed is the safest and most successful method of increase.

Primula × *bilekii*   (H), April, 5cm (2in)
Intense rose-pink flowers with a shining, white eye sit closely over the prostrate leaves. In hotter, drier regions some shade is needed to keep the plant in good health, otherwise it is one of the easiest European types for cultivation.
Propagation. Division of the mat, shortly after flowering has ceased.

Primula   'Blairside Yellow' (E), April–May, 5cm (2in)
A dwarf form of the auricula species, ideally proportioned for the smaller trough. Given a shaded position, the plant will freely produce its umbels of pure-yellow flowers on short stems over soft-green leaf rosettes. A shade-seeker by nature.
Propagation. Division of the clump shortly after flowering has ceased.

103

Primula clarkei   (H), March–April, 2cm (1in)
A charming and delicate little plant for a shaded and humus-rich, acid soil. The dark, glossy leaves appear with the pink flowers, giving the whole appearance a cool freshness.
Propagation. Divide the congested root clusters in autumn.

Primula minima   (H), April–May, 5cm (2in)
The glossy leaves of this squat species are very distinctive. Clustered in neat rosettes, they combine to make up a little tufted mat from which project the bright rose flowers with long, deeply notched petals. The inclination to flower in cultivation varies considerably and it is wise to seek out good clones. Needs a sunny position.
Propagation. As for 'Blairside Yellow'.

Saxifraga burseriana   (E), February–March, 10cm (4in)
One of the finest kabschia saxifrages, raising its large white flowers on red-tinted stems above a neat cushion of narrow, silvery-green leaves. In the hotter, sunnier regions some midday shade is a requirement.
Propagation. Take single rosettes as cuttings in May.

Saxifraga flagellaris   (E), April–May, 5cm (2in)
Golden 'buttercup' flowers stand on short stems raised by groups of rosettes, resembling sempervivums in their form and habit. The plant 'travels' by means of stolons projecting juvenile rosettes to new rooting ground.
Propagation. Simply a matter of detaching young rooted rosettes and replanting or potting them up in July–August.

Saxifraga retusa   (E), March–April, 5cm (2in)
Resembling a scaled-down *S. oppositifolia* in its mat-forming habit and crowded small leaves, this species produces a host of short, upright stems, each topped by pink flower-heads. The red tint in the stem and the starry shape of the flower give the whole plant a refreshing sparkle.
Propagation. Detach rooted shoots in June and grow on as for rooted cuttings.

Soldanella minima   (E), March–April, 8cm (3in)
The daintiest of the 'Snow Bells', with exquisite white, pendant blooms on slender red-brown stalks. They rise from a carpet of tiny round leathery leaves. Not easily persuaded to bloom in warmer, drier gardens, but a lightly shaded trough filled with a cool, fibrous soil can sometimes bring success.
Propagation. Easiest by division of the fleshy crowns in late summer.

Sorbus potteriifolia   Deciduous dwarf tree
Until recently, this naturally diminutive mountain ash was known as *S. pygmaea* and it certainly stays true to that name. In full leaf it stands no more than 15 cm (6in) high. The little blossoms are followed by white, pea-sized

berries and after leaf-fall the fascinating gnarled and twisted 'timber' is revealed. Suitable for the larger trough, with no unusual requirements. Propagation. Autumn sowings of the ripe berries.

Further suggestions for troughs

(NL) indicates lime-free soil needed

Androsace mathildae	White, 2cm (1in), May
Androsace vandellii (NL)	White, 8cm (3in), April–May
Androsace villosa var *jacquemontii* (NL)	Purple, 5cm (2in), April–May
Berberis 'Corallina Compacta'	Orange, 25cm (10in), May
Boykinia jamesii	Carmine, 15cm (6in), June
Calceolaria darwinii	Yellow, 10cm (4in), June
Callianthemum rutifolium	White, 8cm (3in), April
Campanula allionii	Purple, 5cm (2in), June
Campanula arvatica	Blue, 5cm (2in), June
Campanula fragilis	Blue, 10cm (4in), July
Campanula piperi	Lilac, 15cm (6in), June
Cassiope hypnoides (NL)	White, 5cm (2in), June
Cassiope stellariana (NL)	Pink, 2cm (1in), May
Celmisia argentea (NL)	White, 5cm (2in), May
Draba bryoides	Yellow, 5cm (2in), April
Erigeron aureus	Gold, 8cm (3in), May
Erodium chrysanthum	Cream, 15 cm (6in), June–July
Erodium macradenum	Pink, 10 cm (4in), June–July
Fritillaria camtschatcensis (NL)	Purple, 20cm (8in), May–June
Gaultheria humifusa (NL)	Pink, 5cm (2in), June
Gentiana verna	Blue, 8cm (3in), May
Geranium subcaulescens	Red, 10cm (4in), June–October
Hyacinthus azureus	Blue, 15cm (6in), May
Myosotis colensoi	White, 2cm (1in), April–June
Myosotis rupicola	Blue, 8cm (3in), May
Narcissus rupicola	Yellow, 8cm (3in), March
Paraquilegia grandiflora	Blue, 15cm (6in), March
Phlox hoodii (NL)	White, 8cm (3in), May
Polygala chamaebuxus var. *purpurea*	Yellow/rose, 10cm (4in), March–May

Potentilla brauniana	Yellow, 5cm (2in), June–July
Pratia repens (NL)	Violet, 2cm (1in), June–September
Primula auricula var. *balbisii*	Yellow, 5cm (2in), April
Primula × *berninae*	Rose, 8cm (3in), April
Primula bhutanica (NL)	Blue, 5cm (2in), April
Primula frondosa	Pink, 15cm (6in), April
Primula gracilipes (NL)	Pink, 8cm (3in), April
Primula sieboldii (NL)	Rose, 20cm (8in), June
Primula suffrutescens (NL)	Rose, 10cm (4in), July
Ramonda serbica	Blue, 10cm (4in), April–May
Ranunculus alpestris	White, 8cm (3in), May–June
Raoulia grandiflora (NL)	White, 2cm (1in), May
Rhodohypoxis baurii	Purple to white, 5cm (2in), April–July
Sagina boydii (NL)	White, 5cm (2in), June
Saxifraga corymbosa	Yellow, 8cm (3in), May–June
Saxifraga 'Gem'	Pink, 8cm (3in), March
Saxifraga × *kellereri* 'Kewensis'	Lilac, 8cm (3in), April
Saxifraga porophylla	Pink, 10cm (4in), February
Saxifraga sancta	Yellow, 8cm (3in), April
Saxifraga × *kellereri* 'Suendermannii'	Pink, 10cm (4in), March
Scilla autumnalis	Rose, 10cm (4in), October
Shortia soldanelloides [NL]	Pink, 5cm (2in), April–May
Soldanella alpina	Blue, 10cm (4in), April

4 Tufa

Little is known about the first use of tufa for growing plants, or when and where it happened, but the material has certainly been used in the cultivation of alpines for at least 50 years and probably longer; but by no means all of our rock plants can be grown directly in tufa alone and live out their full span with steady growth and flowering. A few respond better to this form of culture than any other.

The tufa we use is not a rock, but a mineral deposit, confined to limestone regions and occurring where rainwater, which has percolated through subterranean limestone, resurfaces as seepage or streams. Its formation has been going on for thousands of years and still is, wherever conditions are conducive. Whilst a detailed description of the chemical processes involved would be out of place in this book, a broad understanding of the happenings helps to explain why tufa is capable of supporting advanced plant life.

In its passage through underground channels, rainwater undergoes an increase in its carbon dioxide content, enabling it to dissolve significant amounts of calcium from the rock. On emergence and meeting with fresh air, the water loses its carbon dioxide enrichment and in consequence sheds some of the dissolved calcium, which forms a solid deposit on whatever the water seeps through, splashes or drenches with its spray. Years of such actions produce a build up of the deposit in a sponge-like structure, of a hardness that varies with conditions. Where the wetting affects a mossy bank, leaf litter or clumps of grass, these can become 'petrified' by the calcium coating. If, in addition, there are periods of reduced flow, further growth or litter builds up on the encrusted material only to be itself subsequently coated and so, layer by layer, a mass of tufa is formed. It is this type of tufa that is sought by the growers of rock plants, as it is usually soft enough to carve for shaping and planting and seems to have the most accessible nutrients for the plants.

Entombed vegetation and other organic matter must contribute to the plant foods held within the tufa and in addition to the calcium, small quantities of other minerals will be included in the deposit. Together with these nutrients, the tufa offers roots a soft granular material riddled with countless pores and labyrinths, the larger of which act as drainage and aeration channels, whilst the smaller ones store long-lasting supplies of moisture. Thus the amalgam formed has a chemical and nutritional balance contained in a structure that is amenable to rooting. This combination is sufficient to satisfy some plants, in particular those species that have adapted to the spartan habitats of rock crevices and screes.

It is said that some lime-hating species will grow in tufa, regardless of the calcium therein, but personal experience has failed to support this claim. From the trials made, a good example is provided by the androsace family, which contains some ideal subjects for tufa culture, with hair-fine root systems and slow, compact, cushion growth. In the family, however, there are two such species which, although staying alive when planted in tufa, fail to flourish and are always stunted and sickly. Both of these inhabit only acid rocks in their natural habitats. Perhaps the contented lime-haters of the reports are not quite so averse to calcium as is believed.

Because tufa is a self-contained growing medium it has been put to use in many modes, one or two of which could be regarded as bizarre, such as the large chunk suspended several feet above the ground from a chain on a 'gallows' structure! On the whole, however, three forms of utilisation predominate; several blocks combined to form an outcrop or growing platform; a single, large block set up as a free-standing garden feature; or smaller blocks used to create a miniature rocky landscape in a trough. Much less common, but highly successful and impressive when well constructed, is the tufa cliff.

Where blocks are used in a bed, whether of a ground level type or of the raised form, their setting up requires special care and attention if plants are to be grown in the blocks as well as around them. The most important factor in this is achieving adequate, but not excessive, moistness within the fabric of the tufa. It is in the winter months when moisture content is most critical, for if the tufa remains too wet after rain or snow-melt it is open to dual dangers. The first of these is waterlogging of the root-runs, which is harmful to the plants, and the second is the consequent risk of frost damage. If the pores and channels within the tufa are overloaded with water, expansion due to freezing can produce ruptures which result in extensive crumbling and flaking. Blocks set deeply in soil are most prone to these dangers; the porous nature of the tufa causes it to absorb surplus water from the ground until it is saturated. Because much of its bulk is buried in wet earth it is unable to shed the surplus and thus remains in this detrimental condition for long periods. In the warmer months of the year a further symptom of excessive wetness is the rapid development of mossy growths on the surface of the tufa and their infiltration of the plants growing there. To avoid or at least minimise such happenings, it is necessary to achieve the right balance between the take-up and loss of water, bearing in mind that the composition of tufa causes it to act like a sponge or wick. If blocks set in beds have only a small proportion of their volume buried in the soil, the much greater volume exposed acts to dispose of excess water by both outward seepage and evaporation. In comparison, the deeply set blocks have as much or even more of their mass taking in water than disposing of it. From experience the optimum for the required balance is for approximately one fifth of the volume to be submerged. The exception to this rough gauge is the scree bed, where retained moisture levels are lower and any tufa incorporated is better sunk to half its depth. If the tufa merely sits upon a surface the capillary mechanism by which it raises water into its fabric is unable to act and too little is retained from rainfall to form reserves for dry periods.

A single boulder of tufa can form an eye-catching garden feature especially when it is studded with plants of appropriate form and habit. Like a trough, it can be mounted on a plinth or squat pedestal, but is then deprived of the moisture supply from the ground and will need frequent attention in watering to keep its plant population in good health. A much more natural and relaxed setting for a free-standing block is one where its base is sunk slightly into a prepared area. The latter is most effective at ground level but if the block must have an elevated seat then this can be formed by a small version of the raised bed. In both cases the seating material is a mixture of chippings and water-retentive substances such as peat, bark or even mineral alternatives like vermiculite and pumice granules. The chippings should comprise about one-third of the mixture to produce a free-draining structure and the remainder is moisture-holding material which the tufa can tap in dry spells to maintain its own water reserves.

Figure 36 A free-standing tufa block with approximately one fifth of the mass below ground

The use of tufa in troughs effectively adds another dimension to planting schemes, giving high places, where plants such as small cascading species can be displayed at their best. It also allows for the contriving of crevices above the general planting level, in which close-growing saxatile types can find secure anchorage. Where the trough, or sink, offers only a small depth, the tufa can be placed directly onto the base and set in the desired position, before the introduction of the filling material. This provides the moisture source for the tufa and also acts to stabilise the arrangements. The ease with which the tufa can be cut and shaped, permits the lumps to be fashioned with a basically flat bottom and to be roughly matched in profile where they touch, eliminating awkward cavities and protrusions (Figure 37).

The compliant response of tufa to shaping, coupled with its light weight, makes cliff building a practical proposition — the only major obstacle for most of us is the cost. Nevertheless, the vertical or near-vertical habitat created, has so much to offer that it warrants description and comment.

Figure 37 Tufa in a shallow trough, bedded with soil mixture

Outdoor cliffs built against earth banks, usually fail due to the action of frost on the over-wet blocks in winter months and erosion by rain in all of the seasons. The successful ones have been erected against walls and in most cases, roofed to give protection from rain, water being supplied in a controlled manner from a built-in system. Figure 38 illustrates the alternative constructions, one being more or less self-supporting through its stepped formation, the other requiring securement to the wall. Neither is in direct contact with the wall, but sits against a narrow infilling of open-structured material with moisture-retentive properties, such as vermiculite or pumice granules, which are coarse enough to allow free passage to surplus water. The bigger the block, the better it forms a component of the artificial cliff, through its inherent stability when cut to suit its position. Little is done to the exposed face of the block, but trimming is needed on the back, and all mating faces, in the fitting for its allotted place. Water is usually introduced to the top of the infilling material, either as a periodic spray or a continuous drip feed. Gravity and the granular make-up of the infilling then act to disperse it to feed the back faces of the tufa blocks.

Structures such as those just described, have enabled dedicated growers to sustain whole colonies of plants that are generally regarded as particularly difficult, even when they are given individual attention in alpine-house culture.

Obtaining and selecting tufa

In limestone districts, with a significant rainfall or heavy winter snow-cover, it is fairly safe to assume that tufa will be present somewhere in some form, although not necessarily of a suitable type. In England's Peak District there are extensive deposits, but mostly of a very hard composition, which will not support plants and require the best stone-cutting equipment to make any impression. In contrast, some coastal cliffs a hundred miles or so away, produce a tufa from saturated turf, which collapses into crumbs under the pressure of finger and thumb.

Ideal formations are neither common nor easily worked and in consequence, tufa is and always has been expensive, when compared with the cost of an equal weight (or mass) of rock. It is possible to discover minor deposits of the right structure and hardness and to build up a stock of small pieces, but on the whole the commercialised quarry is the source of supply and the setter of the price.

The ease with which tufa can be modelled to produce desired shapes and features, has already been mentioned. Of course, this is measured relative to similar tasks on stone, but the tools required are simple and easily used. A coarse-toothed saw, of the type used for logs, will cut through tufa quite efficiently. Chisels with a narrow cutting width fail miserably as shaping tools, as they tend to merely sink into the tufa like a driven nail, but if the blade is wide it will cut and carve efficiently. Masonry drills with very hard cutting tips are unnecessary and in fact the most effective types for boring holes are those used by carpenters. Holes can usually be carved out however using a fern trowel or an old woodworker's gouge. Knocking off unwanted lumps etc. is best done with a wooden mallet which imparts the soft blow that is more effective and kind to the tufa than the steel head of a builder's hammer.

When obtained, quarried tufa is usually covered to various degrees with tufa 'flour' — fine particles of the material that cling to the surface, clogging the pores and when dry, forming a soft cement-like skin. This substance has to be cleaned off and the jet from a hosepipe will do the work very quickly, revealing as it does the textures and features previously hidden. After this cleaning stage, the tufa should be left to shed its surplus water for a day or so, before any further work is done. Ideally, it will benefit greatly from being left to weather for up to a year, but this is a counsel of perfection and few of us have the

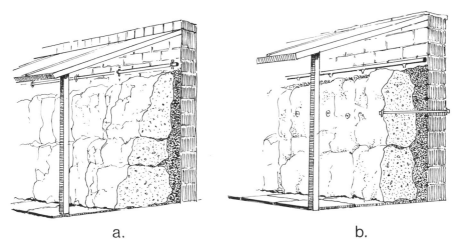

a.   b.

*Figure 38 Tufa 'cliffs' **a**. free -standing, **b**. secured to support wall*

patience to delay gardening projects for so long. Sometimes second-hand tufa is available and it is no less useful or effective than that which is freshly quarried, but it has differences. The effect of weathering on a block of tufa is to harden the exposed surfaces, which is beneficial in that it improves resistance to frost damage and mellows the appearance. But time and weather also bring development of mosses and other small growths to the aged surface, together with unwelcome creepers and crawlers in the niches and tunnels. To make a clean start with such material it can be disinfected, using one of the proprietary fluids based on tar oil and specific to garden usage, but these require a recovery period for the growing medium after treatment, and not surprisingly, there is no guidance on this for tufa. Unless a considerable quantity is involved, an alternative treatment is to pour boiling water over the blocks; not only will this kill both growths and pests, but the tufa is ready for immediate use as soon as it has cooled. The dead material can be removed with a stiff brush.

The internal structure of tufa varies from block to block, and in selecting pieces for planting, whether of new or weathered material, there are one or two indications that help to differentiate the good from the bad. If there are quite a few holes larger than finger size in any one block, these may indicate a coarse structure, with excessive air pockets and oversized labyrinths, making it quite unsuitable as a rooting substance. Conversely, the block may appear to be quite solid, with no airways or pores visible and it could be too dense for rooting. The outward appearance of suitable tufa is that of a finely textured bathroom sponge (of the natural type) and it may well be necessary to clean off the floury coating from new material before this can be assessed. Appearance is not the only basis for judgement, however, for although passing the visual test, some tufa may be too hard or too soft. A pocket-knife will quickly resolve matters; good tufa should carve like soft plaster.

Planting in tufa

Where a single shapely piece of tufa is used as a free-standing feature, the plants are grown *in* it, but if the piece is slightly embedded in soil, they can also be grown *through* it. This alternative greatly broadens the range of plants that can be considered for tufa culture.

Plants grown *in* tufa depend entirely upon the food sources within the substance. The naturally slow-growing, rock-dwelling species find such restriction quite acceptable and grow much as they would in their wild habitats. Of the more vigorous plant types from less frugal homes, a few will make do with the limited supplies, but suffer a stunted and under-nourished existence.

If some planting holes are bored right through the tufa, so that roots can reach the soil beneath, then species with heartier rooting and feeding habits can be included in the planting. With their extra needs satisfied, they still enjoy the benefits of having their vulnerable upper parts in the freely drained, porous tufa and an excellent surface upon which to sit or sprawl.

112

Dealing first with planting *in* tufa, the initial decision to be made is the size of the hole required. If the excavation is made big enough to take the outspread roots of each plant, the tufa will be rapidly disappearing by the time several holes have been made. It is tempting to carve out a small cave, shaped and sized to fit the soil ball of the intended plant and to simply make a transfer from pot to pot-sized hole. But, there is an enormous difference between the growing medium in the nursery pot and the tufa, and it is likely that the roots will be reluctant to explore the harsher substance around them, preferring the easier, richer stuff of the root ball. The usual consequences are that when the food remaining in the potting compost is exhausted, the plant is already weakened and even less inclined to adapt.

In the best interests of the plant, it is necessary to rid the roots of as much of the nursery mixture as can be removed without undue damage. Reduced to a denuded state, the roots no longer have an 'easy' substance to cling to and are faced with a 'tufa or nothing' situation for survival.

To gauge the hole size needed, the tassel of roots should be drawn loosely together, indicating a suitable diameter and depth. If the root length is no more than about 10cm (4in) then a hole of matching depth is a practical proposition; a little kinking and spiral twisting during insertion will take care of a few over-length strands. Roots well in excess of the suggested limit, however, call for a snipping away of the surplus. A diameter of no more than 4cm (1½in) should be adequate for most plants, if they have been properly selected for youth and size.

It is often unnecessary to resort to actual boring tools for the hole-making; an old kitchen knife, pushed and twisted, may burrow into the tufa quite easily. Another piece of cutlery, the teaspoon, is useful for extracting the rubble created as the excavation progresses. If hard spots are encountered, a few blows with a slim chisel should be sufficient to clear them, but if not, or if an internal cavity of some size is revealed, the hole should be abandoned and packed with tufa rubble.

On completion of a satisfactory hole, a planting mixture should be prepared, using tufa crumbs and dry, sharp sand. The plant is then made ready for insertion with the help of a slim fern trowel or a piece of folded card (Figure 39) which will act as a carrier, upon which the plant will be inserted into the waiting hole. Before the trowel or card is withdrawn, the first of the tufa/sand planting mixture can be trickled into the hole whilst the plant is gently agitated. With the hole approximately half filled, the support can be carefully extracted and the filling tamped down with the blunt end of a pencil or twig, taking great care not to tear the roots. At this stage, any required compression of the roots can be commenced, gently pushing them down the hole as further filling is added, progressively pulling the plant closer to the surface of the tufa. When the hole will accept no more of the filling mixture, the plant should be well watered to ensure moisture at the roots, which usually causes some settlement of the filling. A little more of the tufa/sand mixture is then needed to top-up the planting. Finally the plant is secured and the hole roughly sealed, by wedging

113

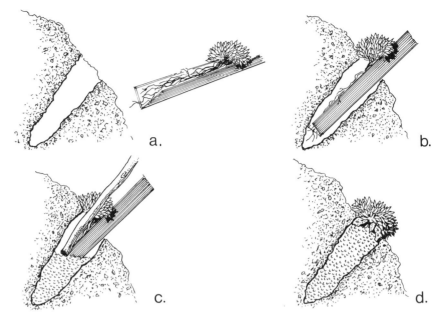

Figure 39 Planting in *tufa* **a**. *young plant prepared for insertion on 'chute'* **b**. *insertion* **c**. *partially filled and tamped prior to chute extraction* **d**. *filling, tamping and capping completed*

flakes of tufa between the neck of the plant and the rim of the hole. It pays to take some trouble in this sealing operation, selecting and paring the tufa flakes, to produce a reasonably good fit.

The technique described is not appropriate for holes that are bored horizontally or nearly so, but then it is strongly recommended that planting holes should always be inclined and in fact are most successful between vertical and 45°. The closer they approach horizontal, the more likely it is that the filling material (and the plant) will fail to stay in place.

It is something of a folly to attempt the establishment of already mature or large plants in tufa; their extensive root systems suffer far too much damage and constrictions. Seedlings poked into small holes are also likely to fail, as their roots are insufficiently developed to withstand the shock and bruising of the planting operation, and they do not possess the reserves to aid recovery. Yearling plants produce the best results, being still small enough for easy handling, yet having enough reserves and stamina to survive the transition. Their youth promotes rapid exploration of the new rooting medium and early establishment.

The *through* hole is planted in a very similar manner, although its diameter and depth may be somewhat greater, to accommodate the type of plant for which it is intended. The excavation is usually vertical or at a steep angle and continues until it breaks through the base of the block. Root shortening is frequently unnecessary, as it is possible and desirable to lead the extremities

114

onto the soil beneath the hole. Insertion of the plant follows the procedure already described, but in this case also includes teasing the roots down to make certain that they contact the soil, if they are of sufficient length.

Through-planting is the method employed for tufa beds, which are a less common form of culture but very attractive and successful when well prepared. The basis is a raised bed filled with a mixture of reasonably good soil, leaf-mould or peat and stone chippings, in the ratio 1—1—2, measured by volume. Slabs of tufa are then fashioned and fitted together, like a rough jigsaw puzzle, to form a complete 'skin' over the entire bed. It is important that each slab should be in full contact with the soil mixture upon which it rests. Joints and cavities between the mating slabs are filled with chippings to complete the skin and the bed is then ready for planting.

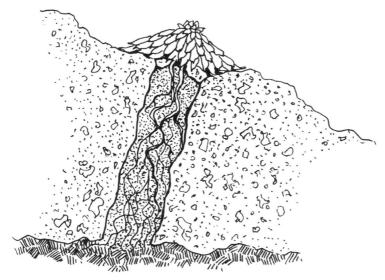

Figure 40 Planting through *tufa, showing the contact of the roots with the underlying soil mixture*

Aftercare

For a few weeks the newly inserted plants of any tufa feature will require regular watering if the weather is dry and also shading in any hot, sunny periods. When new growth becomes apparent these attentions can be relaxed and become part of the care routine used for the surrounding garden. It is not easy to determine when tufa is becoming too dry; its appearance and feel give no clear indications. The safest guide is a check on nearby beds or troughs and if they are needing water, so is the tufa.

Spring is certainly the best time to carry out any planting, when the subjects have the strongest urge to develop. In autumn and winter months the plant suffers some shock and injury when it is much less active and in need of rest. In summer these problems are not present, but watering and shading can demand a lot of time and trouble from an already busy gardener.

Maintenance

When plants do fail to take hold and wither away, their replacement is just a matter of pulling out the corpse, scraping out the filling material and inserting a new plant, in exactly the same way as the original. Established plants require very little attention, other than to be checked for pests. If mosses, liverworts or pearlworts begin to appear on the tufa, they must be dealt with promptly, otherwise they may eventually smother the tight and slow-growing species. Their presence close to, or within, the plant, requires tweezers and patience to pluck them out. Elsewhere on the tufa these nuisances can be kept at bay by scrubbing with a stiff brush. The use of moss-killing chemicals carries a considerable risk of contaminating the plants and is not recommended.

Occasionally, one or two blocks in an otherwise satisfactory batch of tufa will suffer regular crumbling away of the surface, however carefully they have been set up and cared for. The flaw may be only localised or shallow and after a certain amount of loss, a firm surface will begin to emerge, which is proof against the weather and the wound will heal. The crumbling can, however, be a symptom of unsound tufa and will never cease until the whole block is reduced to a pile of crumbs. This is really the luck of the draw and if a block persists in shedding its skin, it should be replaced and crushed up for use in potting mixtures.

Now and again a weed of far more robust physique may invade the tufa, such as a dandelion or willow herb, and if it develops beyond the seedling stage before being noticed, it can present problems in its removal. Very careful use of a hormone weed-killer is the least disruptive method for complete eradication, requiring the liquid or gel to be painted onto the foliage of the weed when it is in active growth.

Tufa requires little else than the tasks described and even these call for only a modicum of energy and pocket-sized tools. Once settled, it can be left to its purpose of supporting its plants and this it will do for many years, supplying their needs sparingly, so that they grow slowly, but healthily, retaining their true scale and character in leaf and flower.

Plants for tufa

Earlier in the text, it was emphasised that tufa culture was only suitable for *some* rock plants. Scale and the manner in which the plants are grown, restrict the selection of subjects to the small and slowly spreading types. As a result the list is considerably shorter than those for raised beds and troughs, where the scope is much wider. The list is further restricted by the decision to admit only plants that will accept a root-run that is entirely tufa, i.e. planted *in* it. Through-planting opens up the choice to include many of the species suggested for troughs.

Anchusa caespitosa   (E), May–August, 5cm (2in)

In the rock garden this plant can produce rather rank growth and few flowers, but when constrained by tufa its true character is preserved. Intense, sky-blue flowers sit in a nest of abrasive, grassy leaves. The white eye of the flower puts the finishing touch to the effect. Shade will not please this native of Crete.
Propagation. Not easy to increase; rooted side-shoots carefully removed and potted up in a very gritty mixture offer the best prospects (summer).

Androsace ciliata   (E), April–May, 5cm (2in)

Much slower growing in tufa than in the more usual pot culture. The cushion of broad-leaved rosettes, produces a wealth of bright-pink flowers with a con-spicuous yellow or orange eye, on short slender stems. Winter cover is beneficial, and essential in wet areas.
Propagation. Seed is usually set in good quantity and germinates well.

Androsace hirtella   (E), April–May, 5cm (2in)

One of the tight, cushion-forming species from the higher altitudes, making a smooth dome of grey-green foliage which can be entirely covered at flowering time. The little white flowers overlap in their abundance and are distinctly almond-scented. A position should be chosen where sun is plentiful, but not broiling. Winter cover is needed in most regions.
Propagation. Collect the easily handled seed in late summer and sow in December.

Androsace villosa   (E), April–May, 8cm (3in)

Tufa culture causes this species to grow in true character, with tightly clustered rosettes in a low cushion and generously produced bloom. Short stalks carry the umbels of white flowers, each with a yellow eye that turns to carmine after a few days, running the tint into the petals. The planting spot should be chosen for plenty of sunlight, and will require winter cover.
Propagation. Seed raising is quite straightforward, or single rosettes can be detached for rooting as cuttings in June or July
Note. The varieties *A.v. arachnoidea* and *A.v. taurica* are equally suitable for tufa culture.

Arenaria tetraquetra   (E), June, 2cm (1in)

A very neat little plant, making a tightly packed wad of foliage carrying starry, white, almost sessile flowers if given a very sunny location. Very slow-growing in tufa and needing a good summer to entice flowering.
Propagation. Take cuttings of single shoots in July or August.

Campanula fenestrellata   (E), June–July, 8cm (3in)
For a sunny chink in a soft tufa, where it will produce a delicate tuft of heart-shaped leaves and strands of massed, cool-blue flowers in summer.
Propagation. Take cuttings of soft growth in March or April.

Campanula garganica   (E), July–September, 10cm (4in)
In tufa the vigour of this species is considerably restrained, even so it is more suited to a large block. Given a position in full sun the plant will produce a tight clump of leafage and a wealth of successive pale-blue, starry blooms for several weeks.
Propagation. Early spring cuttings of new growth.

Campanula tommasiniana   (E), July–August, 15cm (6in)
A delicate looking wiry plant with sparse stems and narrow leaves, flowering in high summer with little pendant, tubular bells of pale blue. Sun or partial shade will be satisfactory.
Propagation. Cuttings of unflowered shoots taken in March or late August.

Campanula zoysii   (H), June–July, 10cm (4in)
In all forms of cultivation this quaint little species is unlikely to live for more than a few seasons and tufa makes no exception. However, on a steep, sunny face it is less likely to be found and devoured by its greatest enemy, the slug. The curiously formed flowers vary considerably from pale to deep blue in the various clones and are carried in crowded bunches just clear of the leaves.
Propagation. Grow a small plant in a pot containing equal quantities of crushed tufa and coarse sand. Divide into rooted fragments in autumn and plant them.

Dianthus callizonus   (E), July–August, 10cm (4in)
Tufa has a slight dwarfing effect on this not-too-easy species. The foliage has a blue cast and is grassy in habit. A conspicuous purple-flecked centre in the large and broad-petalled pink flower, gives the plant special attractiveness.
Propagation. Soft, non-flowering shoots taken as cuttings in June or July.

Dianthus pindicola   (E), June–July, 5cm (2in)
A dwarf species from the Pindus mountains with almost stemless, solitary flowers of a rich pink. The reverse to the petal is buff-coloured, similar to *D. neglectus*. Sharply pointed, silvery leaves make a fine foil to the blooms.
Propagation. Take cuttings of soft, young growth.

Dianthus simulans   (E), June–July, 5cm (2in)
The dense cushion of grey, spiny leaves is studded with flowers of a rich-rose, borne on very short stems. A charming and well-proportioned plant for a sunny spot, although it will accept light shade for some of the day.
Propagation. Cuttings of young growth in July.

Dionysia tapetodes   (E), March–April, 2cm (1in)
Generally regarded, and rightly so, as an alpine-house plant for pot culture, but worth trying. The minute, congested leaf rosettes form a bright-green little mound of foliage which is spangled with tiny yellow 'primrose' flowers. Best sited on the shady side of a tufa block and needing overhead cover throughout the winter months.
Propagation. By seed or single rosette cuttings taken in March. Neither is easy.

Eritrichium nanum   (E), May, 5cm (2in)
A plant of notorious difficulty in cultivation, but, like the *Dionysia*, can be coaxed into growth and flower with tufa culture. The 'forget-me-not' flowers of brilliant blue are in loose heads on short stems radiating from closely growing, hairy leaf clusters. The placing should be sunny, but not baked and never lack moisture in the root-run.
Propagation. Sow fresh seed as soon as it is obtained.

Helichrysum milfordiae   (E), June–July, 5cm (2in)
This silvery-leaved, mat-forming species can be fickle in its flowering, producing an annual display for one gardener and nothing for another using the same cultivation technique. Although a sun-loving type, it will tolerate some light shade for part of the day.
Propagation. Remove rooted offsets in summer and grow them on in pots.

Leontopodium alpinum var. niveum   (E), May, 5cm (2in)
A large-flowered and refined form of edelweiss, shorter in stature than the normal species. The grey, woolly leaves make a base for the stout flower stems and the white, fluffy, 'starfish' blooms with their almost black centres.
Propagation. Sow seed in January, but do not expect abundant germination.

Petrocallis pyrenaica   (E), May, 5cm (2in)
This lovely, soft-toned, low cushion grows slowly and flowers well on tufa, where the creeping stems, clad in their markedly notched leaves, will follow the surface contours. The flowers are a pale, lilac-pink and nestle against the foliage.
Propagation. Easy from seed, or cuttings of side-shoots taken in August.

Phyteuma orbiculare   (H), June–July, 10cm (4in)
The plant has already been described in the list for troughs. It is equally at home in tufa, particularly if occupying a niche between two adjacent blocks, where it will slowly develop and live for many years if its aversion to root disturbance is respected.

Ramonda nathaliae   (E), May, 10cm (4in)
Rather tidier in character than *R. myconi*, with glossier leaves of a fresh green and a flower that is more campanulate. It responds best when planted in a

vertical, or near-vertical face of a tufa block with a slightly shaded aspect. Only young plants should be used (rosette not more than 5cm (2in) across).
Propagation. Sow fresh seeds in autumn and expect to wait three years for a plant of adequate size.

Raoulia lutescens (E), July, 1cm ($\frac{1}{2}$in)

When all else fails, tufa can prove to be quite acceptable to this superb carpeting plant. It competes with the finest moss for density and minuteness of leaf, then excels by producing a sprinkling of little sessile, yellow flowers over its surface in summer.
Propagation. Cut out small, rooted fragments from the edge of the mat in July or August and pot up in very gritty soil.

Saxifraga 'Baldensis' (E), June, 5cm (2in)

This name is no longer valid but is still widely used by nurserymen to describe a form of *S. paniculata* native to Monte Baldo. It can also be found labelled *S. minutifolia*. The mat of tiny, grey leaf rosettes bears sprays of white flowers.
Propagation. Single rosette cuttings in July or August.

Saxifraga caesia (E), June, 8cm (3in)

An ideal plant for tufa, loving a hot position in impoverished limy ground. Its cushion is tight and hard with a pronounced blue cast to the silvered leaf rosettes. Whippy stems hold loose sprays of clear-white flowers. Plants should be chosen in bloom as they vary considerably.
Propagation. Single rosette cuttings taken in June or July.

Saxifraga × edithae (E), March, 8cm (3in)

One of the numerous hybrids from the kabschia group of the genus. Neat spidery rosettes of slightly encrusted leaves form a domed cushion. The rose-pink flowers are in small clusters on short, sparsely leaved stems. Sun or light shade are suitable.
Propagation. Single rosette cuttings in June or July.

Saxifraga 'Faldonside' (E), March, 8cm (3in)

A fine kabschia hybrid with bright yellow flowers of good size and substance. The narrow-leaved rosettes are packed tightly in an attractive domed cushion. Too much sun can scorch the plant, so give it a position tempered with midday shade.
Propagation. Single rosette cuttings in June or July.

Saxifraga 'Gem' (E), March, 8cm (3in)

The flowers of soft pink are solitary, but generously produced and enhanced by a ruby-red eye. In appearance the cushion is very similar to that of *S.* 'Faldonside' and also needs shade from the hottest sun.
Propagation. Single rosette cuttings in June or July.

120

Saxifraga marginata   (E), March–April, 8cm (3in)
A species that forms a rather flat cushion of close, broad-leaved rosettes with silvered edges. The flowers are of the purest white and rise on short stems in profusion. A sun-lover with resistance to drought.
Propagation. Single rosette in June or rooted fragments removed and potted up in July.

Saxifraga retusa, subsp. augustana   (E), April, 2cm (1in)
It is important to ensure that the plant obtained is the true subspecies. The subspecies *S.r.retusa* grows on acid rocks and is not suitable for tufa. In appearance the plant is a dwarfed *S. oppositifolia*, making a creeping mat. In flower it differs, producing starry, rose-tinted clusters on short stems and is a jewel of the genus.
Propagation. Snip off self-rooted stems or take cuttings of side-shoots, in June.

A note on saxifrages

With very few exceptions the European kabschia saxifrages and their prolific hybrids are excellent subjects for tufa culture. This is also true for the majority of 'encrusted' species. There is far less certainty, however, regarding the Himalayan species which are becoming increasingly available, as most are found on non-calcareous ground.

Footnote

Here then is the end of the list for tufa culture. It must not be regarded as complete, but merely a selection of plants which, from personal experience, are amenable to living in that remarkable substance. There will be others, some of which appear likely to thrive from their natural way of life, and a few with far less promise that may respond quite unexpectedly. If the plant is dwarf by nature, needs only frugal fare and is not known to favour only acid terrain, then it might find tufa acceptable. Disregard the current assertions on its cultivation and try it in a freshly carved planting hole — it may give you a pleasant surprise.

5 Pests and diseases

In some respects many of our rock-garden plants are more vulnerable to attack by certain pests and diseases than the majority of garden flowers, particularly those species originating in the higher altitudes, where insects, fungi and viruses common to the lowlands are rare or completely absent. An aphid attack which merely distresses a border plant, may prove rapidly fatal to a mountain species that has never encountered the insect, and consequently has developed no defences against it. The same situation applies even more where fungal and viral diseases are concerned.

To the frustration of the gardener, the alien encounter rarely works in reverse; the slug finds Japanese or American leaves just as palatable as the native herbage and seems to suffer no ill-effects from a diet of 'foreign food', and so it is with the sap-suckers, root-nibblers, bud-rotters etc.

The dilemma for the sensitive cultivator, is to establish a satisfactory balance between destruction and conservation. Many insecticides are indiscriminate, killing the beneficial along with the harmful types, but thankfully the ever-growing concern for the environment is now giving us alternatives with strictly selective action and there is a developing aversion to the general over-use of garden chemicals. Anxiety has driven some gardeners to abandon all synthetic control substances, in favour of 'natural' forms such as pyrethrum extract, which for aphid control has proved to be adequately effective. Unfortunately, there are others, frequently based on old remedies, that make a very limited impression and so fail where the attack of pest or disease is of more than mild proportions. Nevertheless, in suggesting treatment for the ills that are about to be described and discussed, there will be a bias towards the minimising of chemical usage and a preference for methods and substances which are environmentally benign — for which I make no apologies.

The intention was to commence this chapter with pests and to work down from the largest to the microscopic, but what is the upper size limit of a pest? Presumably an escaped circus elephant ambling through the rock garden could be classed as a large pest, as could other people's dogs and cats, wild deer, rabbits and moles. The final decision was to leave out mammals altogether and to regard the creeping, crawling and slithering life-forms as being at the top of the scale.

Leaf eaters

In terms of sheer destructive ability, slugs and snails must surely be classed as champions. Not only do they show a preference for young growth, which has a greater crippling effect on the plant victim, but they always seem to browse on the choicest and rarest species first. Where moisture lingers, between and under stones, beneath seed trays and amongst garden litter, they rest through the daylight hours and dry periods, waiting for suitably damp conditions to make their forays into our treasured plants. Before waging war on them, there are one or two actions that can be taken to keep their numbers down. Any unnecessary items left around in the garden which provide them with shelter, need to be collected up; stones, boxes, pieces of plastic, buckets and the like, all constitute likely shelters and breeding places. The destruction of eggs is an attack on the problem at source and the opportunity arises usually during weeding work when they can be discovered amongst roots and between stones. The eggs are colourless, about 3mm ($\frac{1}{8}$in) in diameter and lie in clusters. A favourite breeding and browsing place is the compost heap, or any pile of rotting vegetable waste. In such places eradication is simply a matter of detection and disposal.

The metaldehyde pellet is by far the most widely used and, alas, *misused* form of control. Many gardeners broadcast handfuls over beds and pathways, creating a hazard for other creatures such as birds, frogs and hedgehogs, which include slugs and snails in their diet. It is difficult to find a completely safe way of using pellets, the main problem lying in the wanderings of the victim after it has taken the bait. The best that can be done is to conceal a few pellets in traps made from hollowed-out potatoes, inverted flowerpots etc.

Liquid preparations that kill by contact and are sprinkled over infested areas, create similar problems of adequate control.

The 'slug pub' presents little risk to anything other than its intended victim. A plastic drinking cup or similar, buried to its rim in the soil and filled with beer, is the lure, and the enticed slug, after presumably drinking its fill, drowns.

A halved and squeezed orange left inverted in the soil has a similar strong attraction. It can be collected and disposed of with the 'catch' inside it.

The surest and safest method requires a little effort and time. It has no side effects and costs nothing. When the weather is ideal for the slug and darkness has fallen, take a torch, an old glove and a small plastic bag — find 'em, bag 'em and get rid of 'em!

Other munchers of leaves, shoots and flowers are the larvae of moths. They are nocturnal feeders and usually seek the softest and newest growth of over-wintering plants. These caterpillars grow up to 4 or 5cm (2in) long and range in colour from bright green to olive brown. Top dressing provides them with an excellent daytime hideaway, where they curl up just beneath the surface, often very close to the plant that they are devouring. Cold weather brings a temporary halt to their activities, but they quickly resume feeding with renewed appetite when the temperature rises again.

Their presence should be suspected where foliage or buds have been eaten, but no trace of slug slime can be found. Watering the affected plant with a liquid derris solution is usually effective and the chemical is amongst the least noxious. The completely safe alternative method of riddance is to catch them at their nightly feasting in the light of a torch and dispose of them.

Only occasionally do day-feeding caterpillars infest alpine plants and even when they do, their attentions are usually concentrated on the larger leaved shrubby types. The finger and thumb are generally sufficient eradicators and there is little need to resort to chemicals.

Last in the list of sizeable leaf-eaters and somewhat less destructive than those already dealt with, but still a pest in some respects, is the woodlouse. It is regarded by some as harmless, eating only dead and decaying vegetable matter, but there is strong evidence to the contrary. They have been seen to gnaw away newly emerged seedlings and plants weakened by transplanting, drought or disease. Little colonies can be found hollowing out tubers, but whether they initiated the damage or merely exploited an existing wound is not clear. Gamma BHC dust is the frequently recommended treatment. For those anxious to avoid the use of chemicals the only practical deterrent is to eliminate the breeding places as far as possible, which essentially requires good garden hygiene.

Earwigs are rare visitors to the rock garden, occasionally found in the dry seed-heads of irises and lilies.

The adult vine weevil certainly eats leaves but its larvae are far more destructive and will feature in the next section.

Root-eaters and other soil pests

Several moth larvae are in this category, most being a dull brown and about 3.5cm (1½in) long; they are mainly discovered during weeding or hand forking. The 'search and destroy' approach is usually sufficient for satisfactory control.

Wireworms and millipedes have a preference for tuberous and bulbous plants, but will also eat other fleshy roots. The only sign of attack may be a small round hole penetrating the skin of the tuber or bulb, yet the interior may be extensively hollowed. The market offers several chemical preparations specified for these pests and if the infestation is considerable there is no equally effective alternative; however, certain plants such as mustard are repellent to them. If practicable, a sowing of these in the area affected can produce a satisfactory clearance.

One of our beneficial centipedes is sometimes mistakenly identified as a millipede and unjustifiably put to death. It is light-orange in colour, about 7cm (2½in) long and has 80 or more pairs of legs. When disturbed, it writhes vigorously.

The vine weevil is a small, dark-brown beetle which nibbles neat holes in a variety of leaves. Its larvae are amongst the worst of soil pests for the rock gardener. The first sign of their existence is often a sudden collapse of what, until then, appeared to be a healthy plant. A post-mortem examination will frequently reveal partial or complete severance of the crown from the root system. The larva is almost white, up to 1.5cm (⅝in) long, with a conspicuous glossy, brown head and it assumes a 'comma' form when disturbed. An old gardening adage says, 'If you find one weevil look for more'. This indicates that very rarely is the grub solitary and several are normally found in the roots of a plant. The larvae attack a range of plants, prominent amongst which are primulas and saxifrages.

It is said that the widespread use of peat-based growing composts is responsible for a great increase in weevil infestations, as the material provides ideal breeding and feeding conditions.

Collected leaf-mould should always be suspected of containing eggs or larvae and treated accordingly.

Our defences against the weevil are poor; several commercial potions make optimistic claims, but perform poorly. The most certain, but disruptive form of chemical-free treatment, is to dig up the affected and suspected plants for a search through their root systems and the destruction of all larvae found there. Otherwise the only treatment accredited with effectiveness is to drench the plant and surrounding soil with a solution of gamma BHC, first making holes in the soil with a dibber to ensure that the liquid reaches the lower root levels.

Another root-eating grub with a similar appearance to the weevil, but three times bigger, is the larva of the cockchafer beetle or may bug. Mercifully it is not often found in the rock garden, but if discovered should be exterminated.

Symphylids look something like pale, dwarf centipedes, about 8mm (⅓in) long and feed on root hairs, with a special liking for primulas. Symptoms of a significant attack are a loss of vigour in the plant and/or wilting in hot weather. The only form of control seems to be the gamma BHC drench.

Aphids are sap-suckers and belong to the next section, but one tribe of that vast and infuriating race, attacks roots instead of foliage and so ranks as a soil pest; it is the root aphid. As with symphylid attack, the plant's distress is signalled by loss of vigour and if the damage is extensive, wilting or collapsing may occur in hot, dry conditions. Affected roots bear what appear to be particles of a white, fluffy substance amongst their fibres and in severe cases, give the impression of being covered in white mould. These effects are produced by the sticky, furry body covering of numerous tiny aphids. Acting as a protective coat, it is also proof against the majority of contact insecticides. Control 'by hand' requires plants to be uprooted and cleared of soil for a brief rinsing of their affected roots in methylated spirit, which penetrates the aphid's coat and kills it. Systemic insecticides do produce impressive results, and as they only harm sap-sucking insects, after take-up by plants, do not have the overkill potential of contact types. It is worthy of note that grasses are host plants to the root aphid, hence specially susceptible plants should be kept clear of weed grasses and lawn edges.

Sap-suckers

Hundreds of species make up the aphis family, but for our purposes those that plague the plants of the rock garden can be regarded as of two types — greenfly and blackfly. Both seem to have equally injurious effects. Their presence can be either quite obvious or hidden. Plants with twiggy or open growth, reveal the aphid colonies clustering on their most succulent parts, but close-growing plants and cushion species can be badly crippled by an unseen horde. In the latter case, symptoms can be a marked 'dulling' in the appearance of the leaves, often accompanied by a slight overall laxness in the foliage. Another clue is a 'sooty' deposit on the leaves, caused by a fungus thriving on the secretions of the hidden aphids. Where it is easy to do so, the finger and thumb can wipe out a multitude in a second, without risk to anything, but not often is it so simple. Leaving the control to natural predators just does not work; even if a ladybird or its larvae could eat a thousand aphids in a single day, it would still take dozens to make any satisfactory impression on a few badly afflicted plants. Some form of spray is the only realistic large-scale weapon. The soft-soap solutions used in Victorian gardening have a limited and temporary effect, needing to be applied rigorously and almost daily to maintain control. Pyrethrum-based sprays, used promptly when attacks are first seen, are efficient and of low risk. Highly selective preparations containing primicarb, are asserted to be harmless to other beneficial insects (by the manufacturers). Systemic types carry some danger to friendly insects during application and whilst drying off, but afterwards only affect anything that is actually eating the treated plant.

Scale insects behave a little like minute barnacles, clinging hard to leaf surfaces and protected from predators (and contact insecticides) by a hard shell covering. They are generally of a light to dark-brown colour and about the size of a pinhead. Extensive infestations are rarely reported and even when they occur, their massed effect seems to cause the plant far less distress than would a similar assault by aphids. It is possible to prise the scale insect away from its anchorage, but at the cost of some damage to the leaf. Where only a few are involved, however, the plant injury is very slight. Serious attacks can be countered with systemic insecticide, applied with care and accuracy.

On sunny days, tiny, bright-scarlet spiders can be seen, dashing frantically around on any smooth, stony surface, with seemingly endless energy and little purpose. They are quite harmless, but because of their colour, thousands are killed every sunlit hour by gardeners who mistakenly identify them as the notorious red spider mite. The real thing is smaller in size and although reddish, has nothing like the brightness of colour possessed by the ill-done-to little spider. The red spider mite is usually more prevalent in glasshouses where the warm, dry atmosphere is much to its liking, but in good summers it may become damaging to some outdoor plants. Fine, light-grey freckling on leaf surfaces is commonly the first sign of an attack which, if allowed to develop, causes leaves to become yellowed and flaccid. Gossamer-like webbings can sometimes be seen, hence the inclusion of spider in the naming of this mite. There are natural predators, including other mites and also cool, damp conditions put a strong restraint on activity and reproduction. Regular spraying with water will check the spread of the pest to some extent. If it is felt necessary to use chemical combat, there are systemic solutions which are quite effective, containing either dimethoate or diazinon.

In the last few years a blight has spread with alarming speed through saxifrages in cultivation, crippling growth and flowers, leading, very slowly, to eventual death. The culprits are parasitic nematodes, too small to be seen and living within the tissues of the plant. They are virulent and all too easily transferred from plant to plant. There are chemicals that can bring about control, but they are highly toxic and quite unsuitable for use by amateurs. Infected or suspect plants should be removed and burnt.

The creature is capable of migrating through the soil to unaffected plants and can also lie dormant, awaiting a new host, so it is pointless to plant replacement saxifrages where victims have been removed.

Moulds

Botrytis, or grey mould, thrives in warm, humid conditions and normally only grows on dead or dying leaves. Placid, moist, summer weather encourages its spread and if left unattended, vulnerable plants can be badly damaged or killed by the rapid advance of botrytis and secondary fungi which it attracts. Asiatic primulas are common casualties. Much can be done to prevent progressive damage if affected foliage is removed by hand and the healthy growth remaining is dusted with powdered sulphur. In severe cases a systemic fungicide may save the stricken plant.

There are soil-dwelling moulds that can cause what gardeners refer to as 'root rot'. They are complex and should not be a problem if the soil mixture has the necessary properties of good drainage and aeration.

Viral disease

It is very difficult for the gardener to even recognise or diagnose viral infections, let alone treat them. Yellowing of leaves can be a symptom, occurring in blotches or a variegated pattern, but such discoloration can also be a sign of bad drainage, root aphid, drought, lack of trace elements and several other plant ailments or deficiencies.

If it can be confirmed that a sickly plant is suffering from a virus, there is unfortunately no cure. It must be disposed of and kept away from healthy plants in the process.

Deficiency-based illness

Lack of sufficient nitrogen is probably the commonest and best-known deficiency in general gardening, but seldom a problem in the cultivation of alpine plants, for reasons given earlier. Another which is also widespread, but less understood is lime-chlorosis, where the presence of significant calcium levels prevents certain plants from taking up essential trace elements. Most ericaceous species are prone to this deprivation and are categorised as lime-haters which strictly speaking is incorrect. Ericaceous plants have evolved on acid soils where lime is not completely absent, but extremely scarce, and they have become super-efficient in taking up the traces that exist. Given what to them is an abundance of lime the systems become overloaded and impaired, the result being lime-chlorosis. Symptoms are leaf-yellowing, declining health and leaf-loss, but as previously noted, any or all of these can arise from other causes.

Magnesium, potassium, aluminium, magnesium and iron are some of the trace elements which, if lacking, can affect the health of plants. It is a complex subject requiring the study of specialised books and articles.

Nuisances

Birds can be a mixed blessing for the rock gardener. In their helpful role they remove pests and add to our enjoyment of the garden, but they can also take a fierce delight in shredding crocus flowers, plucking lumps from cushion plants and tweaking off buds and shoots. Fine netting stretched over growing places works well as protection against winged vandals, but it rather spoils the general appearance and is an obstacle to weeding and maintenance. A less conspicuous deterrent, which hampers work very little, uses the soft, iron, florists' wire usually obtained in bundles of a length that is just right for the intended purpose. Single pieces of the wire are pushed vertically into the soil amongst the susceptible plants, with about two-thirds of their length remaining above ground and a handspan apart. They are so fine and dull in colour as to be virtually invisible and if they are silver and shiny when new they will rapidly rust outdoors to the desired dullness. Whether the bird sees or feels the wires is not known, but it quickly loses interest in the area and suffers no harm at all. The system offers a bonus by being unpopular with cats.

Ants can create extensive damage to a carefully planted bed and totally destroy the contents of a trough. Whilst they probably don't *eat* roots, they must at least chew them in the process of building and extending their living quarters. Whatever does go on below ground, it causes both injury and death to plants. Older remedies include the pouring of boiling water onto the nest, or soaking it in paraffin and setting it alight, neither of which is suitable for planted areas. The sap of the herb Tansy certainly displeases ants and they will not cross a surface wetted with it. Dusting preparations containing pirimiphos-methyl are very effective when sprinkled around the nest's entrance or forked into the earth that it occupies.

128

In the vegetable and flower garden the earthworm is a valued benefactor, but in the carefully prepared mixtures of raised beds and in densely populated troughs, their activities can be troublesome. The unseen damage is a progressive filling of air and drainage spaces by worm excretions plus disturbances to root systems. The visible troubles are the surface casts, forming little conical piles of extremely fine, processed soil and vegetable matter which is very soon spread across the top dressing by the action of rainfall. These smeared casts encourage mosses and weeds, giving them a helpful start to infiltrating the surface of the bed or trough. After sunset, in mild, wet weather, worms can be found stretched out above ground with just a tail-end remaining in the burrow. Caught in this exposed state they can be picked up and deposited elsewhere in the garden, but the action has to be swift and sure, otherwise the worm will swell its anchoring tail to defy extraction. The torch used in the operation should be dimmed by one or two layers of paper over the glass; worms are sensitive to light and will retreat to their burrows with remarkable speed if the searching beam is too bright.

The foregoing has covered only the more common pests and diseases likely to afflict rock plants in the open garden. Others which are less frequently encountered are left to the specialised publications dealing far more extensively with identification and treatment.

Appendix: Sources of Plants and Seed

Most garden centres nowadays have a section devoted to alpines, but there is a sameness about most of them, their stock having been obtained from the same mass-producer source. As a result, from Exeter to Edinburgh the choice varies very little. This is not to say that the species offered are inferior; for the most part they are healthy, well-grown and worth a place in the rock garden, but for the less common and more difficult-to-raise alpines, the buyer must look elsewhere.

Specialist nurseries are few and widely separated. Only one or two operate a postal service and it is normally necessary to make a visit. The wise will obtain a copy of the catalogue before doing so, to avoid disappointment at the journey's end.

An alternative means of obtaining the less common types is to raise them from seed. Some nurseries offer a seed list in addition to their plant catalogue. Expeditions to the mountain regions of the world frequently operate a share system whereby contributors receive a portion of the collected seed. The Alpine Garden Society, the Scottish Rock Garden Club and similar organisations in other countries, feature seed distribution schemes, from which members may obtain a selection for a token cost.

Many enthusiastic growers of alpines are generous with their propagated material, especially when the person seeking plants displays genuine interest and knowledge. The collection of wild specimens is now discouraged with ever-increasing firmness — and rightly so.

The list which follows names and locates some of the most likely sources for the rarer plants and seed.

Alpine plant nurseries (UK)

Those that specialise in alpine-house plants are marked with an asterisk.

*R.F. Beeston, 294 Ombersley Road, Worcester WR3 7HD. (Limited opening hours.)

Blackthorn Nursery, Kilmeston, Alresford, Hants SO24 0NL (*Daphne*, personal callers only.)

Broadleigh Gardens, Barr House, Bishop's Hull, Taunton, Somerset TA4 1AE. (Hardy bulbs.)

Butterfields Nursery, Harvest Hill, Bourne End, Bucks SL8 5JJ. (*Pleione.*)

*Cambridge Bulbs (C.F. and N.J. Stevens), 40 Whittlesford Road, Newton, Cambridge CB2 5PH. (*Crocus, Fritillaria, Iris.*)

*P. & J. Christian, Pentre Cottages, Minera, Wrexham, Clwyd LL11 3DP N. Wales. (*Crocus, Corydalis, Fritillaria, Tulipa.*)

K.W. Davis, Brook House, Lingen, Nr Bucknell, Craven Arms, Shropshire SY7 0DY.

Jack Drake, Inshriach Alpine Plant Nursery, Aviemore, Invernessshire PH22 1QS Scotland.

Edrom Nurseries (Propr. J. Jermyn), Coldingham, Eyemouth, Berwickshire TD14 5TZ Scotland.

Highgates Alpines (R.E. and D.I. Straughan), 166A Crich Lane, Belper, Derbyshire DE5 1EP. (Personal callers only.)

Holden Clough Nursery (P.J. Foley), Holden, Bolton-by-Bowland, Clitheroe, Lancs BB7 4PF.

W.E.T. Ingwersen Ltd, Birch Farm Nursery, Gravetye, E. Grinstead, W. Sussex RH19 4LE.

*L. Kreeger, 91 Newton Wood Road, Ashtead, Surrey KT21 1NN. (Also issues a seed list.)

Potterton & Martin, The Cottage Nursery, Moortown Road, Nettleton, Nr Caistor, N. Lincolnshire LN7 6HX.

M. Salmon, Monocot Seeds, Jacklands Bridge, Twickenham, Avon BS21 6SG. (Bulbous plants, seed list.)

D. Sampson, Oakdene Nursery, Scotsford Road, Broadoak, Heathfield, E. Sussex TN21 8TU.

Tile Barn Nursery, Standen Street, Iden Green, Benenden, Kent TN17 4LB. (*Cyclamen.*)

Waterperry Horticultural Centre, Alpine Dept, Nr Wheatley, Oxon OX9 1JL. (*Saxifraga.*)

Tufa supplies can be obtained from the following company:
Bodfari Tufa Rock, Clwyd Concrete Company Ltd, Bodfari, nr Denbigh, Clwyd, LL16 4DA. (074 575 277)

Commercial seed lists

Jim and Jenny Archibald, 'Bryn Collen', Ffostrasol, Llandysul, Dyfed SA44 5SN, Wales. (Field-collected seed — Europe, Turkey, Northwest USA — also from cultivated stock.)

C. Chadwell, 81 Parlaunt Road, Slough, Berks SL3 8BE. (Himalayan genera.)

Chiltern Seeds, Bortree Style, Ulverston, Cumbria LA12 7PB.

L. Kreeger (see nursery list).

Monocot Seeds (see nursery list under M. Salmon).

Northside Seeds, Ludlow House, 12 Kingsley Avenue, Kettering, Northants NN16 9EU.

Rocky Mountain Rare Plants, PO Box 20483, Denver, Colorado 80220-0483, USA.

Southern Seeds, The Vicarage, Sheffield, Canterbury, New Zealand.

D. & A. Wraight, 25 rue Paul Eyschen, L-7317 Steinsel, G. D. Luxembourg. (Seed collected in the Andes.)

Alpine plant suppliers (USA)

Colorado Alpines Inc., PO Box 2708, Avon, CO 81620.

Lamb's Nurseries, E.101 Sharp Avenue, Spokane, Washington 99202.

Mt Tahoma Nursery, 28111-112th Avenue East, Graham, Washington 98338.

Oliver Nurseries Inc., 1159 Bronson Road, Fairfield, CT 06430.

Rice Creek Gardens Inc., 1315 66th Avenue Northeast, Minneapolis, Minnesota 55432.

Rocknoll Nursery, 9210 US 50, Hillsboro, Ohio 45133-8546.

Rocky Mountain Rare Plants, PO Box 20483, Denver, CO 80220-0483.

Russell Graham, 4030 Eagle Crest Road Northwest, Salem, Oregon 97304.

Siskiyou Rare Plant Nursery, 2825 Cummings Road, Medford, Oregon 97501

Index

Plant index

133

PLANT INDEX

Erythronium dens-canis 66
Euryops acraeus 69

Fritillaria
 camschatcensis 105
 pallidiflora 73
 tubiformis 66

Gaultheria trichophylla 73
Gentiana
 angulosa 101
 kochiana 71
 occidentalis 72
 saxosa 101
 septemfida 60
 × stevenagensis 101
 verna 105
Geranium
 farreri 60
 napuligerum 60
 subcaulescens 105
Geum
 montanum 71
 reptans 64
 × rhaeticum 72
Globularia incanescens 72

Haberlea rhodopensis 60, 73
Hacquetia epipactis 64
Hedera helix 'Marginata' 102
Helichrysum
 angustifolium 71
 milfordiae 119
 sessilloides 102
Hepatica triloba 61
Heuchera sanguinea 71
Hutchinsia alpina 58
Hyacinthus
 amethystinus 66
 azureus 105
Hypericum
 anagalloides 102
 polyphyllum 71

Iberis sempervirens 69
Incarvillea delavayii 71
Iris
 histrioides 66
 reticulata 71
 winogradowii 102

Jasminum parkeri 102
Juniperus communis
 'Compressa' 102

Kalmiopsis leachiana 73

Leucojum autumnale 73
Lewisia
 cotyledon 71
 rediviva 61
Linaria alpina 64
Linum 'Gemmell's
  Hybrid' 61
Lithodora diffusa 69

Merendera montana 67
Morisia hypogaea 72
Myosotis
 colensoi 105
 explanata 65
 rupicola 105

Narcissus
 asturiensis 103
 bulbocodium 67
 cyclamineus 73
 rupicola 105
 'Tête-à-Tête' 71

Oenothera glaber 71
Oxalis
 adenophylla 103
 'Ione Hecker' 72
 laciniata 67

Papaver rhaeticum 61
Paraquilegia grandiflora (syn.
  P. anemonoides) 105
Penstemon
 davidsonii 65
 pinifolius 71
 roezlii 71
 scouleri 61
Petrocallis pyrenaica 72, 119
Phlox
 caespitosa 58
 'Chattahoochee' 61
 hoodii 105
Phyllodoce nipponica 73
Phyteuma orbiculare 103,
  119
Polygala chamaebuxus var.
  purpurea 105
Potentilla
 brauniana 106
 nitida 65
Pratia repens 106
Primula
 auricula var. balbisii 106

× berninae 106
 bhutanica 106
 × bileckii 103
 'Blairside Yellow' 103
 clarkei 104
 edgeworthii 73
 elatior 71
 frondosa 106
 gracilipes 106
 halleri 71
 hirsuta 65
 marginata 62
 minima 104
 × pubescens alba 71
 reidii var. williamsii 73
 rosea 73
 sieboldii 106
 suffrutescens 106
 vialii 73
Pulsatilla vernalis 62

Ramonda
 myconi 73
 nathaliae 119
 serbica 106
Ranunculus
 alpestris 106
 gramineus 62
Raoulia
 australis 72
 grandiflora 106
 lutescens 120
 subserica 65
Rhododendron 70
Rhodohypoxis baurii 106
Rhodothamnus
 chamaecystus 69

Saponaria ocymoides 72
Sagina boydii 106
Saxifraga
 × apiculata 71
 'Baldensis' 120
 burseriana 104
 caesia 120
 cochlearis 58
 corymbosa 106
 cotyledon 72
 × edithae 120
 × elizabethae 72
 'Faldonside' 120
 ferdinandi coburgi 58
 flagellaris 104
 fortunei 62
 'Gem' 106, 120
 'Kathleen Pinsent' 72
 × kellereri 'Kewensis' 106
 marginata 121

134

General index

CAMBRIDGESHIRE COLLEGE OF
AGRICULTURE & HORTICULTURE
LIBRARY
LANDBEACH ROAD, MILTON
CAMBRIDGE   CB4 4DB